Elementary Statistics for Effective Library and Information Service Management

Leo Egghe
and
Ronald Rousseau

INFORMATION MANAGEMENT

Published by Aslib-IMI

ISBN 0 85142 451 1

Information Management International (IMI) is a trading name of Aslib.

Aslib-IMI provides consultancy and information services, professional development training, conferences, specialist recruitment, Internet products, publishes journals (in hard copy and electronic formats), books and directories and provides outsourcing revises to the information community.

Aslib-IMI, founded in 1924, is a world class corporate membership organisation with over 2000 members in some 70 countries. Aslib actively promotes best practice in the management of information resources. It lobbies on all aspects of the management of, and legislation concerning, information at local, national and international levels.

Further information is available from:

Aslib-IMI
Staple Hall
Stone House Court
London EC3A 7PB
Tel: +44 (0) 20 7903 0000
Fax: +44 (0) 20 7903 0011
Email: *aslib@aslib.com*
WWW: *http://www.aslib.com*

Printed by Bell and Bain Ltd., Glasgow

TABLE OF CONTENTS

Preface

Nowadays it is increasingly necessary for an organisation to prove its usefulness, to evaluate its past actions, to justify the need for a proper infrastructure and appropriate personnel for an increasing number of activities. These "necessity proofs" must be delivered by means of reports (such as annual reports) to the parent organisation or other funding body in order to justify, maintaining or developing services.

These reports can only be accurate if the appropriate statistical data, generated by library staff, is accurate. In our experience most librarians have difficulty with statistical methods of generating data. Most of them have had inadequate training on this subject and it generally requires too much effort to learn these methods from existing literature. Indeed the specified literature is vast and often assumes a basic understanding of elementary statistics.

As authors, we have more than ten years' experience, in managing libraries as well as in teaching quantitative techniques to library students. We believe that a simple course on basic statistical applications in libraries is absolutely essential. Hence the writing of this book. It contains most of the answers to the everyday statistical problems librarians face and presents many real life cases we ourselves have encountered during many years of practice.

We strongly hope that this work will satisfy the needs of librarians searching for a simple treatment of statistics and that it will encourage them to tackle the more advanced literature. The book does not require any preliminary knowledge of mathematics or statistics, but we recommend the reader to have access to a statistical software package or at least to a pocket calculator with some statistical functions such as mean, variance and - if possible - regression.

We would like to thank the many colleagues with whom we had several discussions leading to many practical problems studied in this book. To mention them by name would be almost impossible and also includes the risk of forgetting someone. We would also like to thank our own Institutes for their continuous support, not only during the writing of this book but also during all our informetric activities which go far beyond the scope of this book.

Finally the authors would like to thank Mrs. Alison Scammel (commissioning editor) and Kathleen Lyle (editorial consultant) of ASLIB for their help in producing this book and Mrs. Viviane Mebis of LUC for the excellent typing of the text in LATEX.

Leo Egghe
LUC
Diepenbeek, Belgium

Ronald Rousseau
KHBO
Oostende, Belgium

Summer 2000

Introduction

According to Marchionini and Maurer (1995) a modern library is an organised set of resources, which includes human services as well as the entire spectrum of media such as text, video, hypermedia and computers with CD-ROM players. Libraries have physical components such as space, equipment, online connections, collection and storage media; intellectual components, such as collection policies that determine what materials will be included and organizational schemes that determine how the collection is accessed; and people, who manage the physical and intellectual components and interact with users to solve information problems. Many of the activities a librarian is engaged in are not sufficiently known either by users or by the parent organisation. Hence, it is in the librarian's interest to write reports describing all aspects of the library's operation (and make sure they are read). These reports are useful for several purposes.

- They form the basis for a professional management of the library. As such they are also indispensable for the librarian.

- They are a source of information for library patrons. Publicising operations data adds to users' general understanding of a library's complex and time-consuming activities. Consequently, the users are more willing to pay for certain services and show a greater appreciation of all aspects of library work.

- Finally, reports are simply necessary when it comes to convincing parent organisations that the library works efficiently and cost-effectively. They form the basic argument when applying for subsidies for a new service. In times of budget cuts, libraries are especially vulnerable. This is true for university librarians versus the academic and administrative authorities, company and special librarians versus the company's board of directors, as well as governmental librarians versus the responsible minister or civil service department.

A library's activities can be described in a professional manner only by collecting correct and sufficient hard data. But this is not all. According to Menzul (1993), "A mere reporting of the service statistics without meaningful analysis or interpretation relative to the served populations would have little value in helping us to bring our message across to management". Yet all too often library staff are not really familiar with statistical procedures for data collection, analysis and interpretation. This book is written to help them in these matters. We intend to present the necessary

1

techniques in a clear way. All topics covered in this book are described using many real-life examples from librarians' experiences. No mathematical or statistical background is assumed, and this book covers even the most elementary aspects of "library mathematics and statistics".

The first part of the book deals with reports, management aspects, data gathering and the problems encountered with it, especially in an electronic environment. In particular, it describes a number of statistical data a report on the library's activities could (or even should) include. These data can be complete or incomplete. Incomplete data often arise as the result of sampling. For this category of data, simple tips on 'how to sample' are given.

The second part deals with aspects of descriptive statistics. This is that part of statistics that studies practical handling, representation and interpretation of complete or sampled data. Topics studied here include graphical representations, such as techniques for handling a massive number of measurements, scatterplots and regression, calculations of averages, percentiles and variances. Many practical applications illustrate these concepts and techniques.

In the third part we continue the study of sampled data. Indeed, many data are obtained as samples since it is very time consuming, costly or even impossible to collect complete information about certain features. Samples, covering by definition only a part of the totality, present a problem of representability. In this third part we will show, in a simple way, how to draw conclusions for the total collection, on the basis of a sample. Drawing conclusions from samples is called inferential statistics. We will present estimation methods for the average of a certain property, for example the average number of authors of chemistry books or the average number of books per metre of shelf. We will also calculate confidence intervals for these averages. Special attention will be given to the estimation of fractions and percentages (which are fractions multiplied by 100). Examples include the fraction of men, women or children among public library users, overlap fractions between collections, fractions of users preferring certain services and so on. We also give a method for the calculation of appropriate sample sizes in order to reach a certain level of accuracy in the conclusions.

Part 1

Information about the library

1.1 Reports

The ultimate goal of collecting library data is to have at one's disposal useful information about past and present activities in order to prepare for future ones. These data - in streamlined form - and resolutions made on the basis of them will be described in reports, useful for several categories of people:

- Certainly, the head librarian will make management decisions based on these reports.

- Library staff should also have a global view on all library activities and must understand why they have to engage in the daily collection of data.

- Informing library users about the library's activities makes them aware of the reasons why certain rules and limitations are effective and why certain services are not free of charge.

- Making reports public to library patrons and staff is a good way to give them a sense of involvement and to solicit new initiatives and constructive criticism.

- Finally, financing bodies must be regularly informed. This is best done by annual reports.

One could make a distinction between public awareness (PA) and public relations (PR). The activities described in the above paragraph belong to the PA aspect of a librarian's job. Of course, also the PR aspect must be kept in mind. This can be covered by distributing informative brochures amongst patrons, and also electronically on the internet. Moreover, a good librarian has fruitful contacts with the (local) press, thus combining in this way PA and PR aspects.

Returning to the relation between the head librarian and higher bodies, we go now into more detail concerning style and contents of reports. The annual report is the main official document describing and defending the library's mission and how its aims were reached throughout the past year. It relates aims and budgets to results and activities, and forecasts future actions based on a well-studied budget proposal. Special or experimental activities are best described in more detail in occasional reports. Examples of such reports abound:

- informing the library council and financing bodies about the differences in price and delivery times of different booksellers (and suggesting actions on the basis of it),

- reporting on library use during evening or weekend hours in order to optimize staffing, reporting on the use of the intranet and the internet,

- reporting on the use of certain utilities, such as computer terminals, PCs, photocopying machines, in order to know how many are needed, and so on. Certainly, special reports are needed on temporary or experimental services, for example on the use of the internet in the public catalogue area, or on new retrieval software in online public access catalogues (OPACs).

As the name suggests, the annual report is produced once a year at about the same time and covers a twelve-month period: a calendar year, academic year or fiscal year. Do not expect the annual report for a calendar year to be finished in January or even February. Besides time constraints there is the extra complication that the activities of the previous year are not fully concluded at that time, and invoices dealing with the previous year may not be available so soon. This is a typical disadvantage of annual or biennial invoicing. Although it saves time and money (banks charge for money transfers, especially international transfers) it results in financial data being available rather late. From our experience it seems that presenting an annual report in May or June is acceptable. Postponing it further might lead to decreased interest in the report altogether (which might lead to decreases in the library budget!). Moreover, when the librarian has not kept a well-organised diary of all events, postponing can

4

lead to a number of activities being forgotten, especially those for which no numerical data were collected.

Although an annual report should be as complete as possible, it should begin with an executive summary. Members of the board are supposed to read only this summary. The full report is used mainly by the head librarian and for those discussions where full details are necessary. Follow the 'golden rules': be Accurate, be Brief and be Clear. It is obvious why these rules are also known as the ABC rules. Even the executive summary should begin with a one-page abstract where the main conclusions are clearly stated. Reports should not stand on their own but must be related to older ones and to other documents produced by the library, or by the parent body. Trend analyses (evolution of characteristics over time) form an essential part of the presentation. People wanting or needing to know details should be able to find them and to draw their own conclusions if necessary. A conscious use of colour, bold face and italics contributes to the clarity of presentation. Finally, clearly readable tables and figures (such as graphs) should highlight the most remarkable findings (see the next part for a discussion of the graphical aspects of reports).

1.2 Data gathering

No report can be produced without collecting data. These data form the basic material for the librarian. Data are collected by **every** staff member of the library in order to be able to report (yearly) on **all** activities. If services are provided by more than one person, it must be clearly understood what exactly is needed. There must not be a difference of opinion or insight, otherwise worthless data are produced. Examples of possible ambiguity are:

- money spent for books: is it the yearly budget, the ordered amount, the total price of the delivered books, the total price of the invoiced books, or the paid amount in a certain year?

- number of circulations: does this include continuations or not, does it include interlibrary lendings or not?

We mentioned already that data are reported on a yearly basis but the data collection activity itself is an ongoing process throughout the year. Some statistics can be produced at the end of the year, for example, the number of books purchased or catalogued, but this is certainly not the case for the number of books that have been reshelved, the number of visitors, or how many times information to library users has been given. In these cases we talk about daily data collection activities.

What data should be collected? At the end of this section we provide a list of possible topics that could be covered. In this paragraph we will make some qualitative observations. Top priority is the collection of very accurate data even when this implies a reduction in the quantity of data. This depends on the capacity of the specific library. If possible, collaboration with other libraries is advisable. It is interesting to produce uniform statistics per type of library. This yields an additional tool in convincing financing bodies for certain needs, for instance if your library scores lower than a comparable one on a specific topic. Once more, in this case, it is very important that every librarian has the same understanding of all the statistical topics that are covered. Regular meetings on this are in order. Usually, these collaboratively acquired statistics form only a part of the library's statistics.

One of the main uses of data is to study evolution in time: is the number of circulations increasing or decreasing (or constant) over time (despite yearly fluctuations) (see the graphical section in the next part)? How is the number of users evolving, what about the different budgets and so on? In order to be able to draw conclusions over time it is therefore vital that, once a report item is fixed, its meaning does not change over time. Otherwise the numbers are no longer comparable and, hence, conclusions on the evolution in time can no longer be drawn. It should be very clear that, once one has decided to report on a certain new topic (or to change the meaning of a topic) in year x one can only collect the first data in year $x + 1$ and one can only report (for the first time !) in year $x + 2$. It then takes several more years to report on any evolution. Of course there will always be a need for new statistics, for example to report on the use of new technologies. The use of the intranet or the internet in the library is an obvious example.

1.3   Data gathering in an electronic environment

In recent years, the number of "electronic" activities has increased drastically. In most cases this also means that data are gathered in an automatic way and hence there may be a perception that it has become easier to collect data. This is **not** true.

It is true that data are gathered more quickly, but at the same time their accuracy has dropped. One reason can be the fact that these data are delivered by the computer via a third person who might have another insight on the exact definition of a certain attribute. This is even more true when libraries are collaborating in an electronic network. In that case it may happen that quantitative topics wanted by different network partners are not exactly the same as the corresponding ones delivered by the network's computers (and sometimes one even does not know the difference!).

An example is the information on users (based on barcodes): are all users counted, or only the ones that were activated this academic year (i.e. the ones who used the library at least once this academic year). Another problem is reporting on the number of books added to the collection this year: are free books included (e.g. theses), are new editions included, are multiple copies included, how are serials counted, and so on? The problems arise because the data are generated by a computer (and not by each librarian manually) and hence it is not easy to make sure that what is in the librarian's mind is also delivered.

Another reason for the increased problem of automatic data gathering is that during the year there will be some periods of system breakdown and subsequent loss of data. Sometimes this is not observed, sometimes it is and a method of "interpolation" or "extrapolation" is applied, but in any case the final result is not exact. An example is given by unregistered circulations of books.

The problem of data gathering in an electronic environment has been complicated by the increase of web-oriented library activities. A typical example is a web OPAC. Let us give an example from the library of Limburgs Universitair Centrum (LUC). The library catalogue was automated in 1989 and became a web catalogue in 1995. Before this we were able to report on the search time in the library's OPAC. This is no longer possible anymore for the web OPAC. A similar problem is experienced by DIALOG users. Users accessing DIALOG via the WWW find that instead of connect time being indicated (and invoiced in this way), DIALOG units are used instead. However there is no clear definition of these units, and even if there is one (I assume the DIALOG people have a definition!) it cannot be used to measure connect time in a file.

We have come across a major difference between the internet (the virtual world) and the real world: in the latter, "use" is measured by **time**; in the former "use" is measured by **number of contacts**. It is not clear what the impact of such a big change will be on the (social) habits of information exchange.

Even "number of contacts" is sometimes difficult to measure. Let us go back to the example of the LUC OPAC. Since it has become a web OPAC, contact is possible from outside the library and even from any place in the world. It is therefore

- not easy to report on the number of OPAC contacts

- not very relevant to report on all these contacts since an OPAC search, from India, for example, to the LUC catalogue has a different goal than an OPAC search within the LUC library: in the former the OPAC is used as a documentary system in which an information retrieval (IR) process is going on; in the latter the OPAC is often used as a library catalogue.

- Mixing these OPAC searches does not make much sense but separating these different OPAC uses is not possible since, in some (or even many) cases, OPAC searches within the library have an IR goal and are not used to obtain knowledge of the library's holdings.

This is even more the case for a web OPAC search in a university library, performed from a professor's office!

More and more, OPACs serve for IR purposes, thereby partially replacing searches in subject-oriented databases (such as Chemical Abstracts, Inspec, Econlit, ...) often offered by commercial hosts (such as DIALOG). Also the WWW is used as an alternative for these (relatively) expensive IR services. Together with this evolution, there is a move away from services executed by professional library staff to actions performed by untrained users. In addition to this there is the problem of the enormous size of the internet (and of the WWW) and its fast growth (for example see Egghe (2000)). We conjecture that all this implies lower quality of the IR processes (for example in the sense of recall and precision – see again Egghe (2000)) although we must admit that it is extremely difficult to express this in a quantitative way. One major reason for this is that, when searching in the WWW, one does not obtain a clear set of documents but a ranked, truncated list, ranked according to the expected relevance for the searcher. So one can no longer report on "number of documents" retrieved: even "retrieved" becomes a fuzzy notion since, in a search result of say 5 000 documents, the first ones (as presented in the ordered truncated list) are "more retrieved" than the ones on ranks near 100 and these in turn are "more retrieved" than the ones on ranks near 1 000 or 5 000 (these ones are probably not retrieved in the sense that they are not used).

Another problem with web information is that it is usually not dated and often anonymous. This makes it difficult to report here on number of authors, obsolescence of the literature, and so on. Because of the lack of time information, the hyperlinks (clickable buttons) in web pages cannot be considered as the web analogue of classical references or citations (see also Almind and Ingwersen (1997), in which the notion "publication time" is replaced by the notion "real time").

The problems addressed here go far beyond the scope of this book. New, accurate definitions are in order, probably to be formulated as ISO standards by the International Organisation for Standardisation cf. ISO (1991), for this new virtual (but also very real!) world. We must adapt and accept that classical data types (such as connect time) have to be replaced by new data types (such as number of connections). We stress, however, that the statistical methods described in this book apply to all types of data, whether gathered electronically or not. Once good data are obtained, by whatever method, the techniques from this book will lead to a professional management of these raw data, leading to the reports mentioned in Section 1.1.

1.4 Complete and incomplete data

From a statistical point of view, complete data do not exist. All measurements or data gathering activities yield a moment's vision or constitute a sample from a much larger population, such as a library. Nevertheless, for our purposes it is convenient to make a distinction between complete and incomplete data sets.

Complete data are obtained if one wants to report exactly on what one measures. For example:

- The number of borrowings in a year is obviously a complete result. We do not intend to say anything about the circulation behaviour in libraries elsewhere in the world.

- The price of the books that are purchased in a certain year: these are complete data if we only want to report on this. We cannot, however, conclude anything on the price of books elsewhere (e.g. worldwide). If we want to do this, we have incomplete data (so called sampled data) and we have to apply techniques described in the third part of this book in order to draw conclusions.

- The time (in seconds) that the OPAC terminals have been in use in a year. Since we only want to report on the OPAC use in our library, these data are complete.

Most policy decisions are based on incomplete data, that is on samples. Indeed, evaluations and managerial decisions can be made only when there is a vision on the totality in the whole library (or even the world). To know this totality is usually an impossible requirement and one is led to make total conclusions based on a relatively small sample. Some examples:

- The difference in average delivery times between two booksellers can only be estimated on the delivery of books to your library, not on the totality of actions of both booksellers (and often it will even be necessary to sample the books delivered to the library).

- Are there more co-authors (averaged per book) in chemistry than in mathematics? Obviously, only a sample can be taken, certainly when one wants to answer this question in a worldwide vision but probably also within the library since the number of these books might be quite high.

- Asking users' opinions on the library services or asking the population (including non-users) on some library issues will obviously be limited to samples.

In conclusion, one must determine the "universe" Ω: this is the total population (of persons, books, etc.) on which one wants to measure a certain characteristic (cf. the above examples). The size of Ω then determines whether or not we have to draw a sample. Indeed, the size of Ω determines the time (hence the money) we would have to spend on collecting a complete data set. If this is possible, it is clear what to do: we have to measure the characteristics on every element of Ω. If sampling is needed, a lot of time is saved but a new problem arises: how to sample? This is discussed in the next section.

We end this section by introducing tally charts. When data collection is done manually, tallies are made of each observation. A tally is a stroke, and, for the ease of counting, they are grouped in fives. Tally marks are recorded under general headings of a tally chart: see Table 1.1 for an example.

Table 1.1: Tally chart of qualitative data

Attribute	Tallies	Frequency
Language of book		Number of books
English	||||| ||||| ||||| ||||| |||||	25
Dutch	||||| ||||| ||||| ||||	19
French	|||	3
German	||||| |||||		11
Other	||	2

1.5   How to sample

Sampling is something that looks simple; indeed it is simple, but it must be carried out correctly otherwise we end up with what is called a bias. In this section we deal only with the problem of how to sample (the techniques) and leave the problem of sample size to the third part of the book (sizes are calculated using results from that part).

Examples of biases

- A public librarian wants to know what new services might be of interest but a questionnaire is handed out only to present library users.

- Books are picked from a library shelf using a measuring staff or a cord. Thick books have a higher probability of being picked than do thin books, and this might cause a bias, depending on the studied characteristic (certainly the average thickness of the books will be wrongly measured but possibly also other characteristics such as type of book, subject, etc.).

- The time equivalent of the above example: duration of a certain library service is measured at regular time intervals. This yields a bias towards longer services.

- Addresses are picked from a telephone directory; this restricts sampling to people with a telephone (who are not ex-directory).

- Books may be picked from a library shelf by sight, but even this is danger-
  ous: from perception theory it is clear that certain colours (such as yellow)
  are much easier perceived than others. This might cause a bias towards books
  bound in these colours (for example for Springer-Verlag, yellow is the colour for
  mathematics).

These examples help to give an understanding of bias. We can define a sample to be
unbiased if every element in the universe Ω has an equal chance of being included.
Such samples are called random samples and are the ultimate perfection.

1.5.1 Random sampling

In order to perform a random sample we use lists of so-called random numbers to
check that there is no regularity. An example of such a list can be found in Appendix
1, and an extract of it is reproduced here in Table 1.2.

Table 1.2: Extract from a list of random numbers

$$\vdots$$

$$72682$$
$$21443$$
$$\ldots \quad 01176 \quad \ldots$$
$$80582$$
$$13177$$

$$21785$$
$$47458$$
$$\ldots \quad 40405 \quad \ldots$$
$$71209$$
$$85561$$

$$\vdots$$

Such lists can also be generated by a computer, using a statistical software package,
but any such list generated by a computer is in fact a list of pseudo-random numbers.
Perfect randomness cannot be achieved in this way because in the long run computer
algorithms are deterministic. However, for our applications, most personal computer
statistical packages will perform quite adequately.

One can move through such lists in any direction, as long as one keeps going in the same direction. As many numbers as necessary are used. Let us give an example (for didactic purposes numbers are kept small, but they serve as an illustration of how to handle cases involving larger numbers).

Suppose we have a library containing 50 books and we want a random sample of 5 books. First, all books have to be numbered from 1 to 50. It is clear that two-digit numbers will suffice in the table of random numbers. Let us use the list in Table 1.2 from top to bottom, using the two left-most digits of each number. The first number is 72, but this is too large for our sample and hence we cannot use it. The next number is 21, hence we pick the book with number 21. The next number is 01, the first book. Then we arrive at 80, again unusable. We complete the random sample with the books with numbers 13, 47 and 40. The number 21 occurred again, but since this book has been taken already it is omitted this time (it is clear that a random selection implies that each book can be taken once at most). Our random sample therefore consists of the books numbered 1, 13, 21, 40 and 47.

Advantage of the method
The method yields a perfect sample.

Disadvantage of the method
If sampling can be done automatically (by a computer which generates the table of random numbers as well as numbering the books) there is no disadvantage. Of course, things are not always that simple: depending on the purpose of the study one must be able to sample randomly from the whole collection as well as from subcollections (such as medicine, for example).
In addition to this, if we want to measure a characteristic which is not in the computer (for example the number of references in a book), even when sampling is done automatically, we have to go to the shelves and find every selected book.

Manual random sampling is even more time consuming: every book in the library must be numbered. Furthermore, using a list of random numbers with four or five digits (depending on the size of the library) is not easy.

We would like to have a "direct access" method (for instance in a book shelf).

Notes

- When numbering books in the library one must be very careful. Fore some books there is more than one copy on the shelf: do we want to include all copies or not? This depends on the type of characteristic we want to study: if we want to study the average thickness of the books in our library we have to include them all, if we want to study the number of authors we probably do not.

- Books that are not on the shelf (those that have been borrowed, for example) must usually be included in the sample and hence must be numbered.

- Sampling in card files is not so easy since some books have more cards (authors, subjects, etc.) than others.

There are faster sampling methods.

1.5.2   Systematic sampling

Again, we demonstrate the method using the selection of books on the shelf. Selecting, for example 1 book out of 100, is a fairly good method for most problems. We only know of problems with this method in factories where, owing to automatic production processes, for example every 125th product has some defects. If we then sample every kth product we end up with a definite bias, depending on k (sometimes no defects are found, sometimes more than 1 in 125 products has a defect).

However, we do not advise this method since sampling in this way requires counting every book in the library, which is again very time consuming.

Another systematic sampling method is to pick a book every kth centimetre (for example every metre along the shelf). This is obviously a fast method but it yields a definite bias towards thicker books (a 4 cm book has twice as much chance of being chosen as a 2 cm one). This might influence the results: thick books are usually dictionaries, encyclopaedias, student textbooks and so on. So if we want to estimate the fraction of student textbooks in our library, systematic sampling by length is not good.

The time equivalent of sampling by length is sampling by time. If for instance, we want to know the average duration of a service at the information desk or circulation desk and we sample, say, every 30 minutes then there is a bias towards longer service times since they have a higher chance of being included in the sample.

So far we have discussed sampling techniques that are good but time consuming and methods that are fast but yield a possible bias. Fortunately there is an almost perfect and fast method, developed specially for library applications.

1.5.3   The Fussler sampling method

This method, developed by H. Fussler (a former professor in the Graduate Library School of Chicago, see Fussler and Simon (1961)), is beautiful in its simplicity and efficiency. For sampling books on a shelf, for example, it goes as follows. We sample systematically by length using a stick k cm long. The book that is indicated is not picked (as in the case with systematic sampling), but we pick the **next** book. It can be shown (see for example Egghe and Rousseau (1990)) that if the books are arranged randomly on the shelf according to thickness (which is usually the case) the method is as good as the random sample and, obviously, it is as fast as the systematic sampling method. In shelves where books are thicker (such as encyclopaedias and dictionaries) or thinner we can still use the Fussler method as long as we restrict ourselves to these types of shelves (this is a type of structural sampling - see below).

Of course, there is a time equivalent of the Fussler method. When sampling service times at an information or circulation desk, we can check at regular time intervals but record the service time of the next person waiting in the queue (or, if there is no queue, we must wait for the next user to show up).

This method is very important and widely applicable

- in shelves

- on desks

- in computer outputs (for example the length of an abstract received via an online or ondisk search)

- in card drawers (hence we can ignore the differences in thickness between cards and even packing tensions) - see Buckland, Hindle and Walker (1975) for more information.

1.5.4   Structural sampling

This is not a new sampling method, but we apply the above techniques to special parts of a population when we expect differences in the measured characteristic amongst parts and homogeneity within parts.

Put very simply, assume that our library is open 6 days a week and suppose that we know the "weight" of every day with respect to the number of visitors (for example on Saturdays we have 2.5 times as many visitors as on Mondays). Then we must select 2.5 times more people on Saturdays as on Mondays, for example to hand them a questionnaire about library services. Another example, as mentioned in the previous section, is that one can sample structurally in library shelves where special collections are located. For more on this, see Lied and Tolliver (1974).

For sample sizes - a very important aspect of sampling! - we refer the reader to part 3.

We end part 1 by giving some suggestions about topics that can be measured in libraries.

1.6   What to sample

The following list of possible library services is only an indication of what can be done. The list is not exhaustive, nor should it be considered mandatory. Every librarian must determine their own "weapons" of evaluation.

1.6.1   Collection

- Number of books ordered, catalogued, invoiced, possibly divided over several subjects, including the budgets spent.

- Number of series and journals (new, old and discontinued ones), including the budgets spent. Mention if some journals are purchased by so-called library consortia.

- Binding issues, possibly mentioning separately the restoration of books, binding of journals and so on.

- Data on purchases, loan and uses of other products: multimedia publications on CD-ROM, videocassettes, DVDs.

1.6.2   User services

- Mentioning the opening hours including an indication of the use of the library at different time periods (for example in the evening, to see whether or not it is necessary to keep the library open late).

- Circulation data (including renewals, new borrowings, books returned, books reserved) and administrative actions involved with this (sending reminder letters and the subsequent results). Make a distinction between different lending criteria or types of borrowers. Also give statistics on the different subject categories of borrowed books.

- Interlibrary services. Here a lot of statistics can be collected: first of all there are the outgoing and the incoming requests. In each case one can reproduce the success rate (that is the number of satisfied requests divided by the total number of requests). Then mention the weight of each library in these actions, both incoming and outgoing. If possible mention the speed of reaction of each library and also make a financial statement of these actions. Divide between book borrowing and article photocopying and between electronic or hard copy requests/deliveries.

- Photocopy service: how many copies were made? How many printouts of material from a computer?

- Use of the OPAC: total session time (giving an indication on the number of terminals that are needed), average time per session (based on this, one can conclude to what extent the OPAC is used as a bibliographic database). In view of the problems mentioned in section 1.3, "time" might have to be replaced by "number of times".

- Use of external databases (including use of telephone, fax, and so on) online or on CD-ROM (and whether networked). Calculate all costs. Report on the use of the internet (such as the number of connections). Make a distinction - if possible - between the type of library user (for example in a university library: make a distinction between external readers, students, professors, including their specialisations). In general: report on the information technology (IT) activities in the library (such as maintenance of the library's web pages or of the source guide on the web).

- Library facilities and maintenance. How many study places are there? How many books are reshelved every year? This is a typical statistic that informs people about a "hidden" activity that is nevertheless very time consuming. Report on stolen books (or books that can no longer be traced).

1.6.3 Automation and catalogue aspects

- If automation is done in collaboration with other partners, report briefly on their profile and mention the place of your library in the network (fraction of the acquisitions, fraction of the total collection - a comparison of these two data says a lot about the status of your library).

- Indicate the total use of the system (of all PCs and terminals connected to the system).

1.6.4 The personnel

- Describe the employment of the library in persons and FTEs (full time equivalents). Don't forget possible student placements and staff supplied by another department (janitors or maintenance personnel). Describe the organisation chart.

1.6.5 External relations

- Describe the activities outside the library — interlibrary meetings, talks, conferences or other work outside the library — and describe their purpose.

- Report on possible library consortia (for example in the connection of common literature purchases).

- If library staff have been involved in research and have published in journals or congress proceedings, this is the place to mention it.

1.6.6 Budgets

- Specific budgets can be mentioned in their proper location (such as a budget for books). The general budget can be mentioned here.

1.6.7 Data on companies involved in the library's activities

- Reports on the quality of booksellers and of the companies involved with the administration of the journal collection: both price and delivery times are important.

- Reports on the quality of other companies such as binders, computer maintainance firms, office equipment and furniture supplies, and so on.

Try to put all these topics in a time perspective.

There are several documents describing appropriate data gathering topics of interest for libraries, which give accurate definitions and create some standards.

We refer to ISO (1991) and UNESCO (1989) for ISO standards and UNESCO guidelines, Ramsdale (1987) and Ward et al. (1995) for library indicators and management tools proposed by the EU, the ARL (Association of Research Libraries - USA and Canada) statistics and to the international guidelines of the IFLA, Poll and te Boekhorst (1996) for academic libraries. In the UK there is SCONUL (1992) (Standing Conference of National and University Libraries – UK).

The following section is useful for a good understanding of the very nature of the data.

1.7 Measuring scales

Data can be different in nature. We propose the following classification.

1.7.1   Nominal scale

Here, observations are only labels (such as a name). Example: the names of the libraries under study.

1.7.2   Rank order scale

Data are collected according to their rank. Examples: rank order of the performance of several library services, rank order of preferences by library users.

Ranks are numbered 1, 2, 3, ... but they should not be considered as numbers in an absolute sense. Because of the ordering, these observations obviously tell more than a nominal scale. However, the distances between the ranks are not determined. For instance, suppose we know the number of FTE staff members of five libraries, say 13.1, 24.5, 12.9, 17.6, 18.0. If we present only their ranks − 4, 1, 5, 3, 2 − then it seems that the "distance" between each library and the next one in the ranking is the same. The real data, however, reveal that ranks 4 and 5 and also ranks 2 and 3 are very close. The rank order set of data is a very rough estimate; the exact values (called absolute scale) provide the most detailed one possible. Intermediate scales also exist.

1.7.3   Interval scale

The interval scale provides an indication of the differences between the data (without giving absolute data). Example: in temperature measurement, the different scales (Fahrenheit or Celsius) each have a different origin (zero point) and a different unit length. This gives rise to two different scales.

1.7.4   Difference and ratio scales

1.7.4.1 Difference scale

This is the same as 1.7.3, except that the unit length is known. Example: time can be measured using either days or seconds as units.

1.7.4.2 Ratio scale

This is the same as 1.7.3 except that the origin is fixed. Examples: budgets can be measured in different currencies ($, Euro, £, Rs, and so on). The name comes from the fact that, independent of the currency, ratios are constant (for example 18% tax is the same in every currency).

Finally, as already mentioned we have the absolute scale.

1.7.5   Absolute scale

Everything is fixed. Example: counting; the numbers used are the exact quantities one is talking about.

So, the reader should now be convinced that a sequence such as 1, 2, 3, 4, 5 can have many interpretations, from the rank order scale to the ultimate absolute scale.

Part 2

Descriptive statistics

In the previous part we discussed "data" and how to collect them. In this part and the next we will refer to these as "raw data". Indeed, usually one has a large set of numbers and it is important to interpret them: obviously we want to see tendencies, overall properties and so on.

This can be done in several ways, but basically there are two possible goals, once the data are collected.

- We want to present the data in a smooth, streamlined way so that conclusions are easy to draw. Our only goal is then to understand and tell something about the data itself. This is the topic of part 2.

- We consider the data as a sample in a much larger universe. Using this sample we want to draw conclusions about the measured property of the entire universe. This is the topic of part 3 and is not be covered here.

So, in this part of the book we want to present collected data in such a way that they can be located more readily and can be used to facilitate comparisons between different sets. Basically, there are three methods of doing this: using tables, drawing graphs and calculating derived measures. Presenting data in tabular form is relatively straightforward, so we will not cover it in this book but refer the interested reader to Section I.1.1 of Egghe and Rousseau (1990).

2.1 Graphical aspects of data

2.1.1 Mathematical functions

In general a graph is a two-dimensional figure with two axes at right angles to one another. An axis is a straight line with a direction, an origin and a unit of measurement (cf. Section 1.7). The origins of the two axes coincide. In this way, points in the plane are uniquely determined by a pair of numbers (x, y), x being the score on the horizontal axis (called the abscissa) and y being the score on the vertical axis (called the ordinate). See Fig. 2.1.

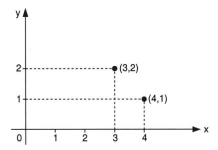

Fig. 2.1: Representation of pairs of numbers as points in the plane.

In mathematics, one wants to represent many points at once. This can be done by using functions, denoted by $y = f(x)$ (y is a function of x), meaning that f indicates the value of y that corresponds to a variable x. We will give an important example. Consider the function

$$y = 2x + 1 \tag{2.1}$$

This equation says that any value x corresponds to a value y which is the double of x plus one. Equations of this type are called linear equations and their graph is a straight line. How is this line determined? It is well known that a straight line is completely determined as soon as we have located two points on it. The line through these two points is the graph we are looking for. In the case of equation (2.1), for example, if we take $x = 0$, hence $y = 1$ and $x = 1$, hence $y = 3$. So two points on the straight line are $(0, 1)$ and $(1, 3)$. Consequently, the graph corresponding to (2.1) looks like that in Fig. 2.2.

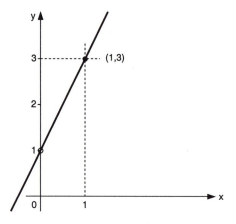

Fig. 2.2: Graph of $y = 2x + 1$.

The general equation of a straight line is

$$y = a + bx \qquad (2.2)$$

where a and b are given parameters. The parameter b is called the slope of the straight line and a is called the intercept. This line is increasing if $b > 0$, decreasing if $b < 0$ and horizontal if $b = 0$ (in this case y is equal to the constant a, see below for an example). In practical examples the variable x often denotes time, and it is then better to replace the symbol x by the symbol t.

Straight lines are the most important mathematical functions. They are obviously also important in our domain.

Example

Suppose the subscription price for a database on CD-ROM is \$2 500 per year and that this database also can be reached online at a price of \$4.20 per access. We simplify this example by supposing that there are no further online costs. What will be the decision of a librarian: to buy the CD-ROM or to continue with the online searches? (We know there are some additional advantages of the online version, for example the fact that it is better updated than a CD-ROM database, but we do not go into this here.) Buying the CD-ROM costs \$2 500, a constant price per year no matter how many times per year ($= x$) it is used. Hence

$$y = 2\,500 \qquad (2.3)$$

is one equation. Online means a cost of \$4.20 per access. Hence the annual cost is proportional to x (= the number of uses per year):

$$y = 4.2x \tag{2.4}$$

The graphs are shown in Fig. 2.3. Buying the CD-ROM database will be the right decision as soon as

$$4.2x > 2\,500$$

hence $x > 595$ accesses a year.

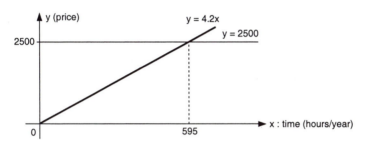

Fig. 2.3: Graphs of CD-ROM and online cost per year.

In conclusion: buy the CD-ROM database as soon as the number of accesses per year exceeds 600.

There are other important mathematical functions (such as exponential functions or logarithmic functions) which are not covered in this book.

2.1.2 Graphical representation of data

Basically, data can be represented in two ways, depending on their nature.

Bar diagrams

Figure 2.4 shows the number of books that have been n years in the library, $n = 1, 2, \ldots$

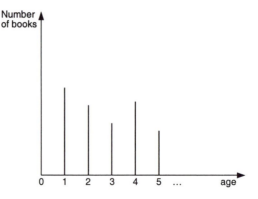

Fig. 2.4: Bar diagram

One could also use a pie chart but a bar diagram is clearer (see the section on perception theory below). Sometimes, for visual clarity the tops of the bars are joined.

Histogram and polygonal curve

For data that are continuous in nature (such as time periods) a bar diagram cannot really be used. The reason is that now measurements are not discrete values (such as 0, 1, 2, ... in the bar diagram) but numbers that are only known to belong to a certain interval. Example: retrieval times or duration of services can be measured in seconds or minutes. As is the case with temperature measurements, the exact time period can never be known but neither is it important. The only thing that interests us is how many cases we find with a corresponding time period between certain values. For example, Fig. 2.5 shows a graph representing the number of OPAC searches with a duration between 0 and 1 minute, between 1 and 2 minutes, between 2 and 3 minutes, and so on. Since the entire numbers of minutes are mentioned in two classes we agree to include them in the second class, for example reporting on the number of OPAC searches with a duration

$$0 \text{ min} \leq t < 1 \text{ min}$$
$$1 \text{ min} \leq t < 2 \text{ min}$$
$$2 \text{ min} \leq t < 3 \text{ min}$$

and so on (i.e. so-called half-open intervals of time $[0, 1[$, $[1, 2[$, $[2, 3[$, and so on). There might be a need to organise a "rest" class, say all searches with a duration $t \geq 12$ minutes (not shown in Fig. 2.5).

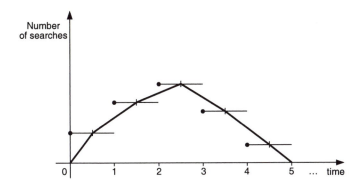

Fig. 2.5: Histogram and frequency polygon

The graph looks like a staircase and is called a histogram. The disadvantage of histograms is that, when we want to present two graphs in one figure, the graph becomes confusing. Therefore, some people prefer not to use a histogram but to use a frequency polygon. This graph is obtained by interconnecting the midpoints of the stairs and closing the curve in the beginning and the end with the value zero (see Fig. 2.5). Now different polygonal curves are possible in one figure by using different thicknesses or colours of lines. Comparison of results is now easier.

Exercises

1. (On bar diagrams). Determine the "age profile" of the library by using the following table of the number (y) of books of a certain age (t) (in years) ($t = 0$ is the present year, $t = 1$ is the previous year and so on). Use, a statistical software package, if possible.

t	y
0	992
1	2034
2	1788
3	1656
4	1457
5	1567
6	1435
7	1232
8	1278
9	1116
10	997
≥ 10	2456

Further exercises can be made by graphing the number of books with 1, 2, 3, 4, ... authors, or the number of books that were borrowed 0, 1, 2, 3, ... times last year.

2. (On histograms and polygonal curves). We have measured the duration of OPAC sessions in the library (in seconds). We found the following results: 67, 108, 135, 35, 47, 89, 127, 86, 44, 123, 167, 101, 144, 82, 307, 262, 103, 153 , 168, 50, 81.
Make the corresponding histogram and frequency polygon.
Note: software packages decide on the number of classes as a default value, but this number can be changed. Try several possibilities and keep the "clearest" graph.

3. The following table, taken from Rousseau and Vandegehuchte (1995) shows the age distribution of available and borrowed books in an engineering library. Draw polygonal curves for the variables "available books" and "borrowed books". Compare visually.

A: publication data
B: number of available books
C: number of borrowed books

A	B	C
[1946 − 1950]	137	14
[1951 − 1955]	267	26
[1956 − 1960]	471	38
[1961 − 1965]	648	79
[1966 − 1970]	886	130
[1971 − 1975]	798	182
[1976 − 1980]	841	232
[1981 − 1985]	693	216
[1986 − 1990]	587	237
[1991−	98	47

Further exercises can be based on retrieval times in commercial online systems, on the duration of circulation actions (or catalographic actions), on response time (in days) in interlibrary lending, on prices of books according to certain price classes, on delivery times of books by some booksellers, or on the age profile of library users, or on the distribution of library users according to the distance between their homes and the library.

2.1.3 Problems with graphical representations

The ultimate goal of using graphs (or figures in general) is to communicate the message in a clearer, quicker and more concise way than is possible by tables or texts. Often, graphs in the literature do not serve this goal. Cleveland (1985) in his interesting book on graphing data found that for instance in the prestigious journal *Science*, 30% of the graphs demonstrated some pitfalls that could be classified as follows:

- construction errors, such as wrong scales

- poor quality drawing

- not enough explanation of the elements in the graph

- drawings too small

Cleveland describes a number of "elementary perceptive tasks" that are required to understand different graphs. In increasing order of difficulty, readers can perceive (see also Fig. 2.6)

- positions of points on a common scale

- positions of points on identical scales, but with shifted origin

- lengths

- angles, directions

- areas

- volumes, curvature

- colours, shadings

That is why pie charts should be avoided: they force the reader to execute the perceptive task of interpreting angles instead of the easier task of comparing points on a common scale (as is the case for a bar diagram). Often one sees placed the corresponding percentages in the pies but this is not a pictoral element and the information could be given in a table!

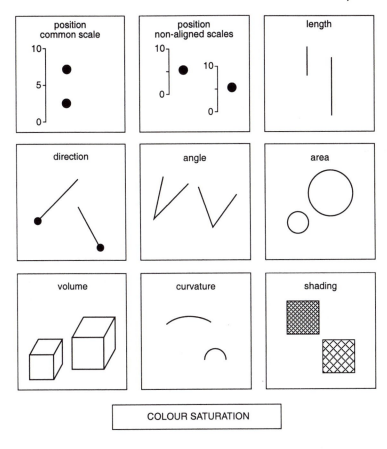

Fig. 2.6: Elementary perceptive tasks (Cleveland and McGill (1984))
(Reproduced with permission from *The Journal of the American
Statistical Association*. Copyright 1984 by the American Statistical
Association. All rights reserved).

Finally we present some general recommendations (Cleveland (1985), Howarth and
Turner (1987)).

- Use good graphs, often they help the reader to understand an article more
  quickly.

- Make good legends and captions.

- Make sure that the details of the graph can be distinguished.

- Do not add too much text **in** the graph, but do not hesitate to add it to the caption.

- Choose the measuring scales to use the available space in an optimal way.

- Make sure the graphs are large enough to stand a reduction - often 65% - when the article is printed.

- When reading proofs of an article, always check the graphs.

2.1.4 Scatterplots and regression lines

When making graphs one often ends up with a large number of points, called a scatterplot. What can we do with such an irregularly shaped graph? For an example, see Fig. 2.7, representing an important case: the horizontal axis represents the time (here years) so that the cloud represents (irregular) evolution of (here) the number of circulations of books per year. In general, however, the x- and y-axis can represent anything (see the examples further on). So, generally, we can discuss here "clouds of points", found as a result of a double measurement (of the two variables). The two selected variables are chosen because we are interested in a possible relation between the two (in our graph in Fig. 2.7, is there a relation between the number of circulations per year and the date; in other words, how is the number of circulations evolving in time?). In all these cases we have an independent variable (on the horizontal axis) and a dependent variable (on the vertical axis).

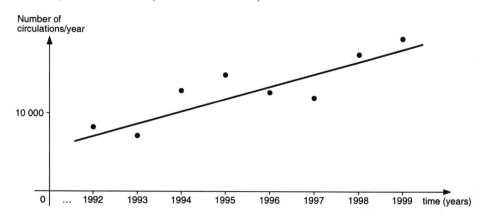

Fig. 2.7: **Number of circulations/year in function of the year**

The slope of the graph in Fig. 2.7 gives the general intuitive idea that the number of circulations is increasing from year to year (in general), although at several points a decrease occurs: in 1993, 1996 and 1997. The easiest way to get some information on this is to consider this scatterplot as a practical approximation of a straight line. Then we are interested in the exact location of this line in the graph. Obviously, one straight line will fit this cloud of points better than others. It is intuitively clear that the straight line drawn in Fig. 2.7 is more or less a "best" fitting line (going "perfectly through" the cloud). How can this line be determined? Recall (Section 2.1.1) that the equation

$$y = a + bx \qquad (2.2)$$

represents any straight line as soon as the values of a and b are known. For the best fitting line, called the regression line, these values can be calculated using any statistical software package or even a pocket calculator (if it has statistical functions). Manually, it takes some work and will be explained in Section 2.2 (for readers who are interested), but we assume here that every reader of this book should have at least a statistical pocket calculator, which will give a and b; the graph must then be produced manually. A computer software package, of course, also produces the graph.

Important remark

The method of calculating regression lines **always** produces a straight line, whether or not this line really fits the data, i.e. whether or not the data show a linear relationship. For testing the quality of the lines that are obtained in the following examples and exercises, we refer the reader to Section 3.8.

Exercises

1. We have the following data on the evolution of the number of incoming inter-library requests for books in our library. ($t = 1$ is the year 1989, $t = 2$ is 1990 and so on)

t	1	2	3	4	5	6	7	8	9	10	11	12
#	467	580	601	487	666	708	814	803	979	1 090	1 211	1 375

Solution
The scatterplot and the regression line are as in Fig. 2.8. The equation of the regression line is

$$y = 313.6 + 77.2t \qquad (2.5)$$

33

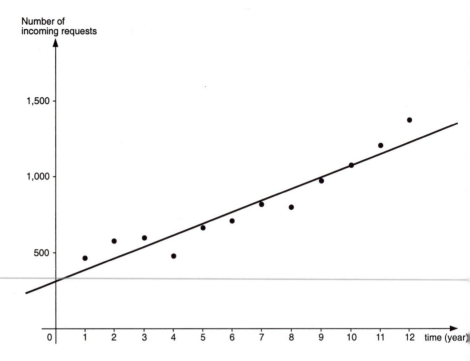

Fig. 2.8: Number of incoming requests in function of the year

We find an increase in incoming requests of about 77 units per year, for the first 12 years. The regression line also allows us to make predictions for the near future: we predict about 1 317 (this is equation (2.5) for $t = 13$) requests in 2001. Of course, there is uncertainty about this; it is only a rough estimate.

2. Suppose we have data on the average number per year a book is borrowed as a function of the age of the book (expressed in years). The data are

t = age	0	1	2	3	4	5	6	7	8	9	10	11	12
y = average loans per year	1.3	1.7	1.6	1.2	1.0	0.8	0.8	0.6	0.5	0.3	0.3	0.2	0.2

Solution
From this table the scatterplot can be determined. Calculation of the parameters a and b yields the equation of the regression line

$$y = 1.57 - 0.13t \qquad (2.6)$$

See Fig. 2.9 for the graph.

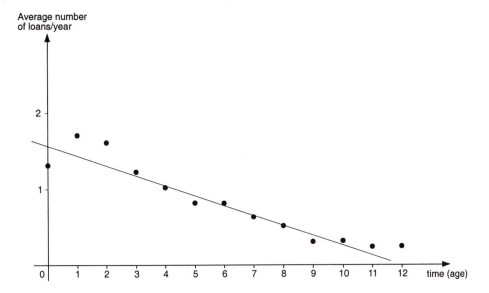

Fig. 2.9: Average number of loans/year in function of the age

We find a decrease of the average number of loans per year of about 0.13 valid for the first 10 years. This could form the basis of a weeding policy.

3. Determine the bar diagram and regression line for the following data, which represent the evolution of the budget of a library (possibly corrected for inflation $(100 = $ year 1991, being $t = 1)$).

t	1	2	3	4	5	6	7	8	9	10
y	100	102.4	106.7	108.1	110.4	112.6	115.2	118.5	121.7	124.5

Solution

The regression line is $y = 97.4 + 2.7t$.

4. We examine 10 libraries and measure

$x = $ budget (in \$100 000)

$y = $ number of circulations per library user (in a certain period)

library	x	y
A	2.30	4.5
B	2.05	4.6
C	3.35	8.2
D	1.95	2.5
E	1.50	2.1
F	2.55	4.9
G	2.00	3.9
H	3.60	8.9
I	3.10	7.7
J	2.75	5.4

Solution

The regression line of y in function of x is

$$y = -3.10 + 3.33x$$

5. Examine the relation between the number of incoming interlibrary requests (x) and outgoing interlibrary requests (y). We have checked 10 libraries. The data are:

library	x	y
A	271	518
B	305	410
C	875	605
D	860	402
E	308	197
F	255	1 078
G	57	320
H	812	592
I	157	34
J	992	860

Solution

The regression line is: $y = 334.2 + 0.34x$, so there seems to be a positive relationship. For a warning on this result, see Section 3.8, exercise 5.

6. Morse presented the following table on the average number of borrowings $N(m)$ of those books in their second year in the library that were borrowed m times in their first year in the library (Morse (1968)):

m	0	1	2	3	4	5	6	7	8	9	10
$N(m)$	0.4	0.7	1.2	1.3	2.2	2.4	2.5	3.7	3.8	4.5	5.1

Solution

The regression line is: $N(m) = 0.18 + 0.47m$.

7. Same situation, now based on the borrowings of mathematics books in the library of Antwerp University.

m	0	1	2	3	4	5	6	7
$N(m)$	0.64	1.11	1.34	2.03	2.61	2.40	1.75	5.00

Solution

$$N(m) = 0.45 + 0.55m.$$

8. The following table gives the approximate number of abstracts (in thousands) in a selection of abstracts together with the cost of each volume (in £):

Number of abstracts	Cost
25.7	160
6.1	78
8.8	107
2.7	50
0.4	19
0.9	26
2.9	36
13.6	83
3.0	41

Is there a linear relation between number of abstracts and cost? If so, estimate the cost of an abstract journal containing 30 000 abstracts.

Solution

We describe the cost as a function of the number of abstracts. This gives:

$$y \text{ (cost in £)} = 29.3 + 5.25x \text{ (number of abstracts in thousands)}$$

The estimated cost for 30 000 abstracts is $(29.3 + (5.25)(30))$ pounds = £186.8.

9. In a public library the journal acquisition budget over the last 6 years is as follows (in 1 000 $):

Year	1	2	3	4	5	6
Budget	280	330	345	360	420	440

Is this a linear increase? If the total library budget in the last year was $800 000 and if this total budget will increase by $10 000 a year, how long will it take before the journal budget takes 70% or more of the total budget?

Solution

We find as the regression line

$$\text{journal budget} = 254 + 31 \times \text{year}$$

Now, in the year 6, 70% of the total budget is $800\,000 \times 0.7 = \$560\,000$. In the year i 70% of the total budget is $560\,000 + (i - 6) \times 7\,000$. On the other hand the journal budget in the year i is estimated at $(254 + 31 \times i) \times 1\,000$. Equating these two expressions yields:

$$560 + (i - 6) \times 7 = 254 + 31 \times i$$
$$\text{or } 560 + i \times 7 - 42 = 254 + 31 \times i$$
$$\text{or } 264 = 24 \times i$$
$$\text{or } i = 11.$$

This means that in 5 years (we are now in year 6) the journal budget will take 70% of the total budget.

This is important information since it means that relatively less money goes to publications (e.g. books) that are more difficult to obtain from other libraries as compared to journal articles, a bad evolution.

10. It is hypothesised that there is a linear relation between the height of the shelf and the number of misplaced books. A test in a library yields the following data. Do these data confirm the hypothesis?

Height above the ground (in cm)	Number of misplaced books
30	21
65	47
100	26
135	32
170	53

Solution

The equation of the regression line is: number of misplaced books $=21.8+0.14\times$

height (in cm), indeed a positive relationship between height and the number of misplaced books. For a warning on this result we refer the reader to Section 3.8, exercise 10.

11. The following table gives the number of users of a public library, grouped per municipality, and the distance between the centre of the municipality and the library. Is there a linear relation between these variables?

Number of patrons	Distance (in km)
1 563	7
1 454	6
554	7
517	9
415	8
389	9
264	12
154	13
128	10
125	16
100	15
77	13
59	20
39	32
39	14
31	14
25	18
20	23
18	18
16	13
11	18
10	26

Solution

The equation of the regression line is:

$$\text{number of users} = 862.1 - 40.37 \times \text{distance}.$$

For a discussion of this result we refer the reader to Section 3.8, exercise 11.

12. The following table gives the evolution in time of the number of library users ($t = 0 =$ the first year that the measurements took place)

t	0	1	2	3	4	5	6	7	8	9	10	11	12
$y =$ # users	234	258	250	297	308	321	304	317	335	370	372	361	382

Solution

The regression line is $y = 244.87 + 11.87t$

Notes

- In most cases it is clear which variable to choose as x and which as y. Remember that x is the independent variable and y is the dependent variable. Reversing the roles of x and y is possible but gives different regression lines and possibly a useless study (e.g. it is clear that the number of circulations must be studied as a function of time, not vice versa!).

- Taking x equal to time (t) yields a simple example of a so-called time series analysis. For more on this, we refer readers to the vast statistical literature on the subject.

2.2 Measuring central tendencies and irregularity of data

In this part we want to find out how to describe the raw data that we have collected. One way of doing this was described in Section 2.1. Another way, as studied here, is to calculate some measures describing central tendency (mean or average, median, mode) and irregularity (standard deviation, variance, percentiles) of these data.

2.2.1 The mean or average

Suppose that the numbers 40, 79, 23, 60, 25, 37, 47, 98, 103 and 111 represent delivery times (in days) of 10 books ordered from a bookseller. If we add these numbers and divide by the number of books (10 here) then we obtain the average or mean delivery time for a book from this bookseller (of course based only on this small sample of 10 books; how to draw general conclusions about this bookseller will be shown in the third part). The mean (average) is thus

$$\frac{1}{10}(40 + 79 + 23 + 60 + 25 + 37 + 47 + 98 + 103 + 111)$$
$$= 62.3 \text{ days (i.e. about 2 months).}$$

In general, when we have N numbers denoted by $x_1, x_2, \ldots, x_N$, the average (or mean) (denoted by $\overline{x}$) is

$$\overline{x} = \frac{1}{N}(x_1 + x_2 + \ldots + x_N) \tag{2.7}$$

$$\overline{x} = \frac{1}{N}\sum_{i=1}^{N} x_i \tag{2.8}$$

From the above, it is clear what $\sum_{i=1}^{N} x_i$ means: we add all the numbers x_i $(i = 1, \ldots, N)$, hence it is $x_1 + x_2 + \ldots + x_N$.

This is a good point at which to remind the reader (if necessary) about the logic of calculations. Multiplications and divisions are executed first, then additions and subtractions. Priority is given to calculations inside brackets. See Appendix 2 for more exercises on this as well as a summary of keys that are available on a pocket calculator.

Although it is very elementary, the mean helps in "smoothing" some graphs. The graph in Fig. 2.10 is taken from Baglow and Bottle (1979) (Reproduced from *Chemistry in Britain* by permission from the Royal Society of Chemistry).

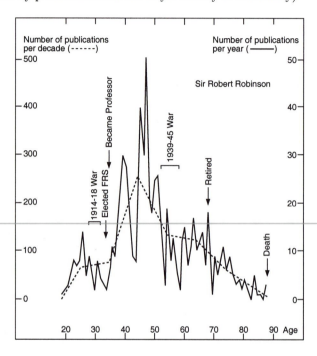

Fig. 2.10: Use of averages in smoothing

It gives the number of publications of an eminent chemist (Sir Robert Robinson), year by year (solid line) and averaged over 10-year periods (dashed line). It is clear that the latter graph is more informative about the evolution of Sir Robert's productivity. In any case, this graph is also much smoother than the first one.

Another way of smoothing data using averages is by calculating moving averages. Let $x_1, x_2, \ldots, x_i, \ldots$ be observed values of a time series, e.g. daily number of loans. We then define f_j as:

$$\frac{x_{j-N} + \ldots + x_{j-1} + x_j + x_{j+1} + \ldots + x_{j+N}}{2N + 1}$$

i.e. the average of $(2N+1)$- values centred at x_j. Usually $N = 1$ or 2, so that averages are calculated over 3 or 5 values. This procedure reduces occasional highs or lows in a data set and makes a general trend more conspicious.

42

When a time series is used for forecasting then the average is calculated over the M most recent data:

$$f_t = \frac{x_{t-1} + \ldots + x_{t-M}}{M}$$

The value f_t is then used as a prediction, based on past data. Note that here the forecast moves by replacing the oldest observation by the most recent one.

Exercise

The numbers of fiction and non-fiction volumes issued monthly to readers of a local public library were recorded. The results were as follows:

Year	1999				2000							
Month	Sep	Oct	Nov	Dec	Jan	Feb	Mar	Apr	May	Jun	Jul	Aug
Fiction	65	105	131	159	151	161	112	179	100	161	205	163
Non-fiction	59	185	322	415	396	467	492	465	598	398	497	512

Use three-point moving averages to describe these data. Draw figures using all data and using only these averages. Observe the smoothing that has occurred.

We now return to the data on the bookseller's delivery times and consider a new set of data: other books ordered from another bookseller and their delivery times:

$$53, 58, 67, 70, 60, 65, 55, 58, 49, 88.$$

We leave it as an exercise to the reader to check that here $\bar{x} = 62.3$ days also, the same as for the first data set. However, it is clear that the second data set is much more regular than the first one. How can we express this?

2.2.2   The variance and the standard deviation

The variance (denoted as s^2) of N data $x_1, x_2, \ldots, x_N$ is calculated as

$$s^2 = \frac{1}{N} \sum_{i=1}^{N} (x_i - \bar{x})^2 \tag{2.9}$$

or, which is the same,

$$s^2 = \frac{1}{N} \sum_{i=1}^{N} x_i^2 - \bar{x}^2 \tag{2.10}$$

43

The positive square root of s^2 is called the standard deviation and is denoted by s. Note that pocket calculators can easily compute square roots. Formula (2.9) says that we have to take the average of the numbers $(x_1 - \overline{x})^2, \ldots, (x_N - \overline{x})^2$ which indeed measure irregularity by checking how the numbers $x_1, \ldots, x_N$ deviate from $\overline{x}$ (smaller or larger — both cases are equally important in measuring irregularity). Formula (2.10), yielding the same value, is more handy for practical calculations. It says, expressed in words, that the variance is the average of the squares of the $x_1, \ldots, x_N$ minus the square of the average of the $x_1, \ldots, x_N$. Of course, a software package or a statistical pocket calculator only requires us to key in the data $x_1, \ldots, x_N$. The variance s^2 can also be calculated manually: we give the calculation for the first example. Make a table of $x_1, \ldots, x_N$ and one of $x_1^2, \ldots, x_N^2$. Find the total in both tables and divide by N. We get $\overline{x}$ and the average of the $x_1^2, \ldots, x_N^2$. This number minus $\overline{x}^2$ is s^2: see Table 2.1.

Table 2.1: Manual calculation of $\overline{x}$ and s^2

i	x_i	x_i^2
1	40	1 600
2	79	6 241
3	23	529
4	60	3 600
5	25	625
6	37	1 369
7	47	2 209
8	98	9 604
9	103	10 609
10	111	12 321

$$\sum_{i=1}^{10} x_i = 623 \text{ days} \qquad \sum_{i=1}^{10} x_i^2 = 48\,707$$

$$\overline{x} = 62.3 \text{ days} \qquad s^2 = 4\,870.7 - \overline{x}^2 = 989.41$$

$$s = 31.45 \text{ days}$$

The measure s for the first example is thus 31.45 days. The same calculation for the second example yields $s = 10.53$ days. From this it is clear that s and s^2 measure the difference in regularity between two data sets very well. It must be stressed, however, that the real importance of s and s^2 will become clear in the next part.

They will be needed (together with $\bar{x}$) in order to tell us something about the whole population. For conclusions about the sample itself, there is a better way to describe (ir)regularity, namely percentiles.

2.2.3 Median, quartile, percentile

We look again at the first example in section 2.2.1. Write the numbers down in increasing order:

$$23, \; 25, \; 37, \; 40, \; 47, \; 60, \; 79, \; 98, \; 103, \; 111$$

For $j = 1, 2, \ldots, 99$, the j th percentile P_j is this delivery time (possibly interpolated) in which $j\%$ of the books are delivered. For $j = 25$ this is called the first or lower quartile (Q_1), the time needed to deliver a quarter of the ordered books. For $j = 50$ it is the second quartile (Q_2) or the median (Md). For $j = 75$ it is called the third or upper quartile (Q_3).

The median is the time period needed to deliver half of the ordered books and hence can also be considered as a measure of central tendency. In any case, all these percentiles P_j give information on the (ir)regularity of the deliveries. Of course, one usually restricts oneself to the calculation of P_j for $j = 10, 20, 25, 30, 40, 50, 60, 70, 75, 80$ and 90.

Without a statistical software package it is hardly possible to calculate percentiles, unless the number of data is not too high. We will give two examples of manual calculations.

Example 1
The data above are put in "cells" or "boxes" as in Fig. 2.11 with an origin and measuring unit below it.

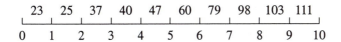

Fig. 2.11: Delivery times and percentiles

25% means $0.25 \times 10 = 2.5$, being in the third box, hence $Q_1 = P_{25} = 37$ days.

50% means $0.50 \times 10 = 5$. This is exactly between two boxes. In this case we take the average of the values occuring in these two boxes: $P_{50} = Q_2 = Md = \dfrac{47 + 60}{2} = 53.5$.

75% means $0.75 \times 10 = 7.5$, hence $Q_3 = P_{75} = 98$.

Other values are $P_{10} = 24$, $P_{90} = 107$, again averages. If we do the same for the second example we find $P_{10} = 51$, $Q_1 = P_{25} = 55$, $Q_2 = P_{50} = Md = 59$, $Q_3 = P_{75} = 67$, $P_{90} = 79$.

The first bookseller delivers 25% of the ordered books in 37 days, whereas the second bookseller needs 55 days to do this. In less than this (53.5 days) the first bookseller even delivers 50% of the ordered books!

Note

The average is a less important measure here. Indeed, in any book order, there will be a few that are delivered very late (for various reasons). They have a substantial effect on $\bar{x}$, and $\bar{x}$ says nothing of how fast some subpackages are delivered. The percentiles solve this problem. Of course, $\bar{x}$ is very important (and even more important than the percentiles) when we deal with the characteristic "price" of a book!

Example 2

We have two sets of delivery times of interlibrary material, coming from two different libraries. The data are (in days)

> A: 25, 37, 15, 58, 101, 70, 90, 5, 8, 22, 36, 47, 3, 26, 18, 71

> B: 43, 52, 60, 30, 29, 52, 62, 40, 54, 35, 48, 27, 26, 21, 32, 48, 55, 64.

Note that these sets are not equal in length: this is not required.

Calculate P_{10}, P_{20}, $P_{25} = Q_1$, P_{30}, P_{40}, $P_{50} = Q_2 = Md$, P_{60}, P_{70}, $P_{75} = Q_3$, P_{80} and P_{90} for both libraries and draw your conclusions.

Solution

For A, put the 16 data in ordered cells as in Fig. 2.12.

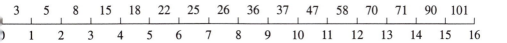

Fig. 2.12: Delivery times of example 2A

For P_{10} : $0.1 \times 16 = 1.6$, hence $P_{10} = 5$

For P_{20} : $0.2 \times 16 = 3.2$, hence $P_{20} = 15$

For P_{25} : $0.25 \times 16 = 4$, hence $P_{25} = Q_1 = \dfrac{15 + 18}{2} = 16.5$ and so on, and the same for B (18 cells now).

We reach Table 2.2.

Table 2.2: Percentile results for A and B

	A	B
P_{10}	5	26
P_{20}	15	29
$Q_1 = P_{25}$	16.5	30
P_{30}	18	32
P_{40}	25	40
$Md = Q_2 = P_{50}$	31	45.5
P_{60}	37	48
P_{70}	58	52
$Q_3 = P_{75}$	64	54
P_{80}	70	55
P_{90}	90	62

Library A delivers 25% of the requests within 16.5 days (about 0.5 month) while library B needs 30 days (1 month) for this. In one month (31 days), library A delivers 50%; library B needs 1.5 months for this (45.5 days). Then library B becomes better: it delivers 75% in 54 days while A needs 64 days for this. The difference is even larger for P_{90}: 3 months for A and 2 months for B.

Example 3

The age profile of the users of library A is as follows (we show a very small number of users here, for practical reasons):

23, 10, 12, 47, 35, 38, 50, 61, 22, 24, 66.

We have

$$
\begin{aligned}
P_{50} &= Q_2 = Md = 35 \\
P_{25} &= Q_1 = 22 \\
P_{75} &= Q_3 = 50 \\
P_{10} &= 12 \\
P_{90} &= 61
\end{aligned}
$$

For library B we have the following (again too small) set of data:

53, 37, 33, 41, 50, 60, 43, 38, 29, 37, 28, 49.

Now we have:

$$
\begin{aligned}
P_{50} &= Q_2 = Md = 39.5 \\
P_{25} &= Q_1 = 35 \\
P_{75} &= Q_3 = 49.5 \\
P_{10} &= 29 \\
P_{90} &= 53
\end{aligned}
$$

Discussion

In library A, 50% of the users are younger than 35 years; in library B this is only so for 25% of the users. In A, 25% are younger than 22 years. Library B also has a higher P_{10} but a lower P_{90} than A.

We hope that the reader is now convinced of the power of percentiles in the calculation of the (ir)regularity of data.

Note

$\bar{x}$ and Md are measures of central tendency. A less used measure of central tendency is the mode, denoted by M_0. This is the value that occurs most often. Some other (less important) measures of central tendency exist, such as the geometric mean

$$
G = \sqrt[N]{x_1 x_2 \ldots x_N} \tag{2.11}
$$

(the N th root of the product of the $x_1, x_2, \ldots, x_N$, where all x_i are non-negative) and the harmonic mean

$$H = \frac{1}{N} \frac{1}{\sum\limits_{i=1}^{N} \frac{1}{x_i}}. \tag{2.12}$$

We do not go into these measures here, although they can be very useful in other applications (see, for example, Egghe, Rousseau and Van Hooydonk (2000)).

The measure

$$V = \frac{s}{\overline{x}} \tag{2.13}$$

could be considered as a relative standard deviation. Indeed, if we have a table of prices in one currency and we transform the data into another currency, s is changed (for example if we have to multiply by 2 (the multiplication rate of the two currencies) then s is multiplied by 2), while the value of V remains the same, as it should. The same goes for other transformations (for example length measurements or time measurements). V is called the variation coefficient. See Egghe and Rousseau (1990) for more on these so-called concentration measures.

2.2.4   Applications: box-and-whisker plots, 80/20 rule, Lorenz curves

Box-and-whisker plots

The dispersion of data can be visualised by using so-called box-and-whisker plots. Such a plot consists of a rectangle (the box) beginning at the first quartile and ending at the third. It is divided into two (generally unequal) parts by the median. This box has two 'whiskers', i.e. two straight lines, one beginning at the 10th percentile (first decile) and ending at the box, (the 25th percentile), and one begining at the box, (the 75th percentile) and ending at the 90th percentile (9th decile). The remaining data, consisting of those points in the first and the last decile, are drawn individually. Fig. 2.13 shows a box-and-whisker plot for the data of the first example.

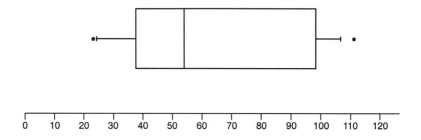

Fig. 2.13: Box-and-whisker plot

Box-and-whisker plots are handy tools for visual comparison of different data sets. This is done for the two previous examples. This graph makes it very clear that the first set of data is much more dispersed than the second one (see Fig. 2.14).

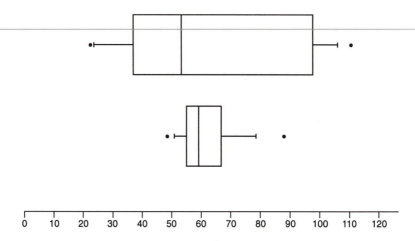

Fig. 2.14: Box-and-whisker plots showing different dispersion of two data sets

The 80/20 rule

The 80/20 rule is a rule of thumb which states that the top 80% of all actions are carried out by the top 20% of all providers. For example about 20% of all centres used for document delivery by a particular library provide 80% of the documents and the top 20% of all library users borrow 80% of all borrowed books. This is an interesting rule between percentiles which shows in a cogent way how a relatively small group determines a much larger part. It has, for instance, been shown (Lowenberg (1989)) that about 20% of all shelves contain 80% of all misshelved books. Knowing which shelves these are likely to be (the bottom ones are good candidates, see Beltaos and Rousseau (1996)) allows library assistants to minimise their work to obtain a maximum result. Of course, the 80/20 rule is only a rule of thumb. In reality, for some services it is perhaps a ratio of 15 to 80, or 30 to 60. We will next see a graphical tool to find the exact relation.

The Lorenz curve

We present a real-life application (Rousseau (1992)). Table 2.3 shows the available number of CDs in a local record library and the number of loans during the year 1990.

Table 2.3: Availability and 1990 loans of CDs in the public library of Puurs (Belgium)

Category	Number of CDs	Number of loans
CLASSICAL MUSIC		
Orchestral	595	1582
Concertos	340	649
Soloists (instr.)	313	627
Ensembles	151	185
Vocal, secular	639	1120
Vocal, religious	330	563
Various	107	395
NON-CLASSICAL MUSIC		
Spoken recordings	148	764
Amusement music	1274	5615
Film music	427	2290
Jazz	491	817
Pop	2549	17510
Ethnic music	235	339
Country and folk	244	672
Various	475	1387

We first consider the loans per category. Ranking loan data from highest to lowest yields the following sequence:

17 510, 5 615, 2 290, 1 582, 1 387, 1 120, 817, 764, 672, 649, 627, 563, 395, 339, 185.

Now we calculate cumulative partial sums, that is the number of loans in the highest category, the sum of the first and the second category, the sum of the first three categories and so on. This gives the following sequence:

17 510, 23 125, 25 415, 26 997, 28 384, 29 504, 30 321, 31 085, 31 757, 32 406, 33 033, 33 596, 33 991, 34 330, 34 515.

We see that the total number of loans equals 34 515.

There are 15 categories, so the first 4 categories constitute 27% of the total number of categories. These 27% of the categories give rise to 26 997 or 78% of all loans. This means that we have here a 78/27 rule. Of course, we could similarly consider the first three categories and conclude that, for these loan data, there is a 74/20 relation. Note that the number 74 comes from $(25\,415/34\,515) \times 100$.

The Lorenz curve of these data is the curve which connects the points with coordinates

$(0, 0), (1/15, 17\,510/34\,515), (2/15, 23\,125/34\,515), (3/15, 25\,415/34\,515),$
$(4/15, 26\,997/34\,515), ..., (15/15, 34\,515/34\,515) = (1, 1).$

See Fig. 2.15. It is now easy to read a $100y/100x$ rule from this curve, where you can choose $100y$ (80, for example) or $100x$ (20, for example) and read (estimate) the other number from the Lorenz curve.

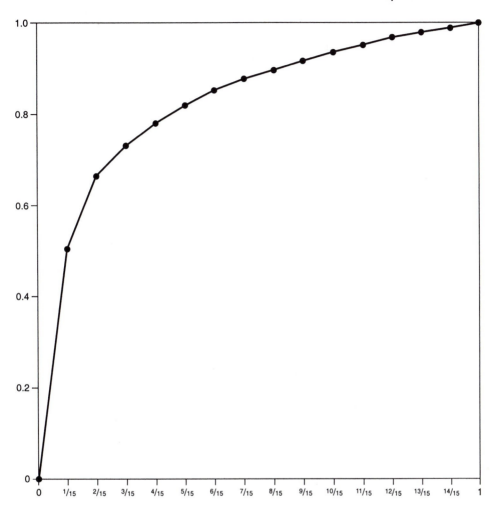

Fig. 2.15: Lorenz curve of loans per category

We now do the same for the availability categories.

We obtain the following decreasing availability sequence:

2 549, 1 274, 639, 595, 491, 475, 427, 340, 330, 313, 244, 235, 151, 148, 107.

The corresponding sequence of cumulative partial sums is:

$$2\,549, 3\,823, 4\,462, 5\,057, 5\,548, 6\,023, 6\,450, 6\,790, 7\,120, 7\,433, 7\,677,$$
$$7\,912, 8\,063, 8\,211, 8\,318.$$

Consequently, this Lorenz curve connects the points with coordinates:

$$(0,0), (1/15, 2\,549/8\,318), (2/15, 3\,823/8\,318), ..., (1,1).$$

Here we have a 78/47 relation, indicating a much more balanced situation. The Lorenz graph illustrates this more clearly. Generally, the more the Lorenz curve approaches the diagonal the more balanced the situation is: the diagonal corresponds to a 80/80 situation. A 'real' 80/20 relation indicates a very unbalanced situation. Yet, (20/100, 80/100) is only one possible point of the Lorenz curve, so that this graph contains much more information than giving an $80/100x$ or $100y/20$ relation.

Here the availability curve is situated completely under the loans curve (see Fig. 2.16). This means that overall availability is more balanced than loans. Usually, one uses a different terminology and one says that lending is more concentrated than availability. Note that it is possible for the Lorenz curves to cross. In this case one computes the coefficient of variation — the ratio of the standard deviation and the mean. The larger this number, the larger the concentration (or the smaller, the more balanced). Here we obtain a coefficient of variation of 1.083 for the availability data and of 1.853 for the loan data (check this as an exercise), using formula (2.13).

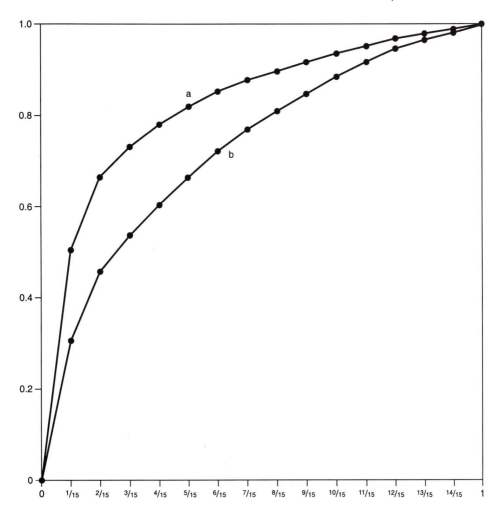

Fig. 2.16: Lorenz curves of loans (a) and availability (b) per category

Exercise

We present a table showing the number of users and the number of overdue books they have. What percentage of users is responsible for 80% of all overdue books? This means that we want to find $100x$ for a $80/100x$ rule.

Number of overdue books:

$$0, 1, 2, 3, 4, 5, 6, 7$$

Number of users:

$$404, \ 96, \ 50, \ 39, \ 20, \ 10, \ 5, \ 1$$

Answer

We have an exact 80/20 rule.

Exercise

Compare Lorenz curves of salaries of library employees in corporate libraries and public libraries and make conclusions about possible differences in salary inequalities.

We close this section with another application of the mean and the variance, namely the calculation of the equation of the regression line of a scatterplot. This part is not necessary to follow the rest of the book and hence can be omitted.

2.2.5   Calculation of the equation of the regression line

We recall from Section 2.1.4 that for a scatterplot one can calculate a best fitting straight line. Such a line has an equation of the form

$$y = a + bx \tag{2.2}$$

and is completely determined once a and b are known. We present the formulae here and give an example.

Let $\{(x_1, y_1), (x_2, y_2), \ldots, (x_N, y_N)\}$ denote the coordinates of the points. Then b is given by the formula

$$b = \frac{\dfrac{1}{N} \displaystyle\sum_{i=1}^{N} x_i y_i - \bar{x} \cdot \bar{y}}{s_x^2}, \tag{2.14}$$

where s_x^2 denotes the variance of the x-values, hence

$$b = \frac{\dfrac{1}{N} \displaystyle\sum_{i=1}^{N} x_i y_i - \bar{x} \cdot \bar{y}}{\dfrac{1}{N} \displaystyle\sum_{i=1}^{N} x_i^2 - \bar{x}^2} \tag{2.15}$$

(cf. formula (2.10)). The other parameter a is given by

$$a = \bar{y} - b\bar{x} \tag{2.16}$$

with b as in (2.15).

Example

We work out exercise 4 in Section 2.1.4. We represent the x- and y-data and add to it the table of x^2, y^2 and xy values.

Table 2.4: Calculations for a and b

Library	x_i	y_i	x_i^2	y_i^2	$x_i y_i$
A	2.30	4.5	5.29	20.25	10.35
B	2.05	4.6	4.20	21.16	9.43
C	3.35	8.2	11.22	67.24	27.47
D	1.95	2.5	3.8	6.25	4.88
E	1.50	2.1	2.25	4.41	3.15
F	2.55	4.9	6.50	24.01	12.50
G	2.00	3.9	4.00	15.21	7.80
H	3.60	8.9	12.96	79.21	32.04
I	3.10	7.7	9.61	59.29	23.87
J	2.75	5.4	7.56	29.16	14.85
$\Sigma \rightarrow$	25.15	52.7	67.39	326.19	146.33

Hence we have

$$b = \frac{146.33/10 - (2.515)(5.27)}{67.39/10 - (2.515)^2}$$

$$b = 3.33$$

and

$$a = 5.27 - (3.33)(2.515)$$
$$a = -3.10$$

Yielding

$$y = -3.10 + 3.33x,$$

a positive relationship between x and y ($b > 0$). The other exercises can be done in the same way.

Part 3

Inferential statistics

3.1 Goal of part 3

In this part we will continue to work with a set of data which we will denote by $\{x_1, x_2, \ldots, x_N\}$. Its mean is denoted by $\bar{x}$ and its standard deviation is denoted by s. In part 2 we contented ourself with studying this set and giving some characteristics of it. However, there is a need for more. Let us show this by giving an example. Suppose the data are on delivery times of books by a bookseller and suppose we find a value of $\bar{x} = 90$ days. Suppose also that, from earlier analogous tests, we know that $\bar{x}$ used to be around 2 months. We then go to this bookseller and tell them that there must be an improvement in the service. Then two things will happen. The bookseller will say first that there is a constant effort to improve services, and then that the tested N (say 50) books are just too small a set in order to state that services have deteriorated. What can we do about this?

Another example. We want to prepare our budget requests for next year. One element in it is the purchase of library shelves. We can estimate the need for this according to the number of books that will be bought and the average thickness of books. We sample, for example 100 books in the library and we find an average thickness of $\bar{x} = 2.45$ cm. How certain are we that this number will approximate the real "library" average thickness, denoted by μ, which we do not know.

In the first example, the "real" value μ cannot be measured since we can never know the real average delivery time of books, averaged over all books provided by this bookseller. In the second example it is possible to know the existing value of μ for the library (but that is too time consuming) but that does not really help for all new books that will be put in the library - so also in this case μ is not known.

Is there a way to estimate μ, based on the sample $\{x_1, x_2, \ldots, x_N\}$? Yes there is, and it does not even require more work: the sample $\{x_1, x_2, \ldots, x_N\}$ is there already and we will show that a very small additional calculation will yield such a total population conclusion.

In this way the bookseller cannot argue that we are only talking about a sample, and a professional conclusion can also be drawn in the case of thicknesses of books. Putting such elements in a report will hence make it much more professional and less vulnerable to criticism than we would expect if we only applied the techniques of part 2.

3.2 First test for the mean: one sample and one set of measurements

First of all we must stress here that this section - although it has some interest in itself - is only a preliminary section for the next three sections (at least) in which the more spectacular methods and examples will be given.

We explain this first technique by means of an example. There is a "rule of thumb" in libraries that, on the average, there are 30 books per running shelf metre (for fully occupied shelves, of course). A sample of $N = 125$ m of fully occupied shelves in my library gives me 125 numbers $x_1, x_2, \ldots, x_{125}$ (each being a number of books on 1 m of shelf) with average $\bar{x}$ and standard deviation s. We only need $\bar{x}$ and s here, e.g. $\bar{x} = 33.3$ and $s = 12.7$. So in my library, at least according to this sample, I found an average of 33.3 books per running metre. Of course, $33.3 > 30$ but it could be that another sample might have given me another number (possibly even under 30). Can I conclude that, based on my sample, in the whole library there are significantly more than 30 books per shelf metre (on average) or must I conclude that the deviation of 3.3 is just an accident? In the first case I take an "active" decision by rejecting the rule "30 books per metre, on average" and will adopt the norm (for the time being) of 33.3; in the second case I take a "passive" decision by not rejecting the value of 30 (although this has not been proved for my library). Note the difference between the active decision of rejection and the passive one of not rejecting ($\neq$ accepting!).

Note too that we require only a conclusion on the "real" $\overline{x}$ of the population, which we have called μ, proposed here to be 30 (the value under study) and not on the complete distribution of the variable "thickness of books". This is the strength of the problem. No matter how the property itself is distributed, the average $\overline{x}$ is distributed as a normal (Gaussian) distribution function. What does this mean? It means that if we perform a lot of samples - such as the one above - (we do not have to do this in practice; it is just a thought experiment to explain the method) we know that they are scattered over the x-axis according to a curve as presented in Fig. 3.1 with μ as the central abscissa. This result is called: the central limit theorem (CLT), and it is the basic theorem of statistics. It is applicable when the value of N is 30 or more (see note at the end of this section).

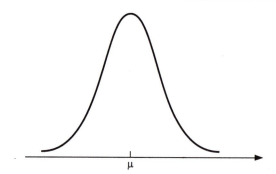

Fig. 3.1: Distribution of the averages $\overline{x}$ of samples

Figure 3.1 illustrates the fact that the closer an observed $\overline{x}$-value is to μ, the higher its probability of occurrence.

We go back now to our original question: is $\overline{x} = 33.3$ significantly deviating from $\mu = 30$ or is it just by coincidence? The decision depends on where in the curve 33.3 is situated. If it is in a "tail" of this curve, the Gaussian distribution says that there is too little chance for this to happen and hence we will reject $\mu = 30$ for our library (active decision). If 33.3 is situated in the "middle part" of the curve (the part with high probability) we will say that the deviation is not large enough and hence that it is not significant and we will keep $\mu = 30$ (passive decision).

So that we are not obliged to produce tables for every new example we reduce every problem to the so-called standard normal distribution, which is a Gaussian distribution with 0 in the middle and a certain standard thickness – see Fig. 3.2.

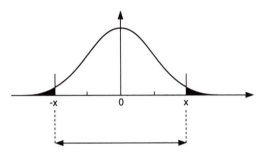

Fig. 3.2: Standard normal distribution

This reduction requires the calculation

$$Z = \frac{\frac{\overline{x} - \mu}{s}}{\sqrt{N-1}} \tag{3.1}$$

or

$$Z = \frac{\overline{x} - \mu}{s}\sqrt{N-1}. \tag{3.2}$$

This gives a point on the x-axis in Fig. 3.2. The method is only valid if the sample size N is 30 or more. This is due to the fact that the model in fact supposes an infinite population; population sizes below 30 then require a correction (which we will not discuss here). Since this curve is completely fixed we can see if Z is in the tail or not. The tail can be defined in several ways but here we restrict ourselves to two possibilities. Note that the total area under the curve in Fig. 3.2 is 1 (since it is a probability distribution). The first method of determining the tail is requesting that the middle part occupies 95% of the area (hence has an area equal to 0.95). The limit x-value is then 1.96. Another method of determining the tail is requesting that the middle part has an area of 0.99 (99% of the area). The limit x-value is now 2.575. The choice between these two alternatives is a matter of experience and will also depend on the type of problem: if a problem is critical, such as changing booksellers, we had better make sure that our conclusions are true for 99%. Otherwise we can content ourselves with a 95% sure conclusion. Other critical values are available (for other confidence levels) in the form of a table, but we do not use it here for reasons of simplicity. A statistical software package informs the user automatically of the other critical values and corresponding confidence levels.

Here is the conclusion for our example:

$$Z = \frac{\overline{x} - \mu}{s}\sqrt{N-1}$$

$$Z = \frac{33.3 - 30}{12.7}\sqrt{124}$$

$$Z = 2.89.$$

Since $2.89 > 2.575 > 1.96$ we can conclude that $\overline{x} = 33.3$ deviates too much from $\mu = 30$, so we reject $\mu = 30$ for our library, and continue to work with $\overline{x} = 33.3$ (active decision). This conclusion is more than 99% sure.

Note that s is also involved here as well as N and $\overline{x}$ (as might be expected, since it is a question about the mean). It is too early here to talk about sample sizes but it is already clear from formula (3.2) that the higher the value of N, the more easily we will be able to reach an active conclusion (if the deviation s from μ is constant of course). Also - as is also clear intuitively - the more regular the data (the lower the value of s), the easier we will be able to conclude actively (since s is in the denominator).

Why are the probabilities of 0.95 and 0.99 taken so high? The reason is that we only want to take an active decision (deviating from the "norm") with a high degree of confidence. The complementary values (0.05 for $P = 0.95$ or 0.01 for $P = 0.99$) give an upper limit for the chance that we might be wrong. In statisticians' language, it is an upper bound on the probability of error. A probability of 0.01 is a 1% chance of error; 0.05 is a 5% chance. Since it is important to avoid such a mistake, we make sure that P is as low as possible, hence that the complement $1 - P$ is as high as possible, and in any case at least 0.95.

This is a long story for an easy procedure. Note that we work with the same tool as in part 2: the sample. The only additional work is the calculation of formula (3.2) and simply concluding whether a deviation is significant or not. A few more examples now follow.

Exercises

1. We measure the number of authors of $N = 40$ books on mathematics and take the average. We find the mean $\bar{x} = 1.7$ and standard deviation $s = 5.5$. We wonder if this deviates significantly from the value of $\mu = 2.3$ that we have read in a publication dealing with books on chemistry.

Solution

Calculate

$$Z = \frac{\bar{x} - \mu}{s} \sqrt{N - 1}$$

$$Z = \frac{1.7 - 2.3}{5.5} \sqrt{39} = -0.68$$

Since the standard normal curve is symmetrical we will be in a tail if and only if $-Z$ is in a tail. Hence the minus sign does not matter, so we use $-Z = 0.68$. But $0.68 < 1.96$. Hence we are not in the 5% tail (let alone in the 1% tail). We conclude that the difference is not enough to say that in mathematics there are significantly fewer co-authors than in chemistry.

Note

Suppose our data were such that $N = 40$, $\bar{x} = 1.7$ but $s = 1.2$. Now $Z = -3.12$. Since $3.12 > 2.575$, we now conclude that $\bar{x} = 1.7$ is significantly lower than $\mu = 2.3$ and hence that there are fewer co-authors in mathematics books than in chemistry books. This example makes clear the crucial role of s; comparing $\bar{x}$ and μ is not enough. This is a mistake that is often made by non-professional workers in the field.

2. We have read in a publication that the average length of abstracts in a certain database is 79.56 words. We now check the German language abstracts separately. A sample of 31 German abstracts yields an average length of $\bar{x} = 67.47$ words with $s = 24.8$. Is this difference significant? In other words, are German abstracts significantly shorter (in terms of number of words) than general abstracts (all languages together)?

Solution

$$Z = \frac{67.47 - 79.56}{24.8} \sqrt{30} = -2.67$$

Since $2.67 > 2.575$ we conclude that the difference is indeed significant.

The reader should now be convinced that the method is not hard to apply. Most of the work is collecting the data, which is necessary anyway, even for the "lower level" applications of part 2.

3. I know that a library user in my library visits the library 12.4 times per year, on average. I would like to know if this average remains the same if I consider only female users (or only users of age 18 or lower, or some other subcategory). A sample ($N = 178$) in this group yields $\bar{x} = 14.7$ and $s = 10.8$. Is the difference significant?

Solution

$$Z = \frac{14.7 - 12.4}{10.8}\sqrt{177} = 2.83$$

We conclude that the difference is significant.

Note on fractions

In this book we will use the term fraction for the number representing the relative size of a subset with respect to the total set, and hence it is a number between 0 and 1 (so we do not use the term fraction in the sense of a rational number in arithmetic). Multiplying a fraction by 100 yields a percentage. For example, the fraction of the books in my library published in 1990 is 0.03 (or 3%). Note that not every number between 0 and 1 is a fraction. A measurement such as temperature of $0.6°$ C is not a fraction!

Fractions express the part of the population that belongs to a certain subset of it. Fractions can be binomial (0–1, yes–no, male–female) or multinomial. Put simply, we can think of fractions as pieces of a pie: the pie can be divided into two pieces (binomial) or more than two pieces (multinomial). Examples of multinomial fractions are the fractions of the library users divided according to gender and 10 age classes (so the pie is cut into 20 pieces), the fractions of the books in the library according to their language, and so on.

Unless otherwise stated, we will always assume we are working with binomial fractions. Fractions can be interpreted as averages ($\bar{x}$) as follows. Suppose we investigate the library users according to gender. We wish to determine the fraction of female users. To do this, we give every male user a score of 0 and every female user a score of 1. The average $\bar{x}$ of all these scores (on a sample of size N) is then the fraction of female library users. It is important to remember that we can treat a fraction as an average since it allows us to apply the test for the mean in this section. In the case of a fraction, we do not have to calculate s: for fractions $\bar{x}$,

$$s = \sqrt{\bar{x}(1 - \bar{x})}.\qquad(3.3)$$

Exercise

I know that the fraction of female users in my library is 60%. I now wonder if this fraction of female users is the same if only persons under 21 are considered. A sample on $N = 200$ yields a fraction $\bar{x} = 0.55$. Is there a significant difference?

Solution

For fractions, using (3.3), (3.2) becomes

$$Z = (\bar{x} - \mu)\sqrt{\frac{N - 1}{\bar{x}(1 - \bar{x})}}.\qquad(3.4)$$

Note that (3.4) is the same as

$$Z = (\bar{x} - \mu)\frac{\sqrt{N - 1}}{\sqrt{\bar{x}(1 - \bar{x})}}\qquad(3.5)$$

but it is more accurate in the calculation (and quicker) if we use (3.4) (in (3.5) we perform one more square root and in addition to this, the square root is in the denominator, giving rise to larger rounding-off errors). So we use (3.4), which yields

$$Z = (0.55 - 0.6)\sqrt{\frac{199}{(0.55)(0.45)}}$$

$$Z = -1.42$$

Since $1.42 < 1.96$ we say that the difference is not large enough in order to talk about a structural (significant) difference.

About the requirement that N must be larger than 30

$N \geq 30$ is required in order to have a good approximation of the distribution of $\bar{x}$ to the normal distribution in the central limit theorem (see the beginning of this section). If $N < 30$, then corrections are needed (using so-called t-distributions). We do not present them here for reasons of simplicity and since it is not really necessary to explain them: if calculations are performed by a software package, these corrections are executed automatically. Furthermore, in most cases, $N \geq 30$ is reachable.

Example for $N < 30$
In a metropolitan area, university, public, governmental and corporate libraries form a network for document delivery. The mean number of books received by interlibrary loan, calculated over all member libraries, was 2 485 (over some fixed period). The number of books received by corporate libraries were:

$$4\,811 \quad 6\,295 \quad 3\,565 \quad 5\,793 \quad 2\,793 \quad 3\,025 \quad 3\,753 \quad 3\,454$$

Is the mean number of books received by corporate libraries significantly different from the mean for all members of the network?

Note that this is a situation where one naturally has a small sample ($N = 8$, since there are only 8 corporate libraries).

Solution
From the above data we find $\bar{x} = 4\,186.1$ and $s = 1\,215.1$. We calculate, as usual,

$$\frac{4\,186.1 - 2\,485}{1\,215.1} \sqrt{7} = 3.70$$

Using the normal distribution we decide on a significant deviation at any reasonable level: the 95% critical level is now 2.365 (instead of 1.96) and the 99% critical level is 3.499 (instead of 2.575), but the system will automatically compare with these (higher) values. When the calculation is performed manually one needs to check certain t-tables, but we do not go into this here.

Another "natural" example where $N < 30$ is, for example, the analysis of the degree of acidity of old paper in an archive. Performing $N \geq 30$ chemical lab tests would be too costly!

About one-sided tests
In all arguments given above we used two-sided tests for the mean $\bar{x}$. This means that we investigated whether or not $\bar{x}$ is in **one of the tails** of the normal distribution, hence whether or not Z (see formulae 3.1 or 3.2) is in **one of the tails** of the standard normal distribution. In exceptional cases we can exclude one of the tails since the situation it describes cannot occur. For example, if one knows for sure that an average article in chemistry cannot have fewer co-authors than an average article in

mathematics one could only check whether or not the average number of co-authors of chemistry articles is **larger** than the number for mathematics articles. The same applies for "natural things", for example public libraries have more circulations than university libraries, scientific libraries have more outgoing interlibrary requests than public libraries and so on. Beyond the library, examples are heights of men and women, temperatures in different seasons of the year, and so on.

One must, however, be very careful when adopting one-sided tests. A one-sided test is not allowed just because we find $\overline{x}$ (the sampled mean) for example to be larger than μ (the hypothesised mean). Only arguments based on logic (or perhaps on long experience) allow us to exclude $\overline{x} < \mu$.

If we can apply a one-sided test it is clear that the total area of both tails is divided into two in order to obtain the area of one tail. More concretely (if $N \geq 30$) the critical value of 1.96 is used for 97.5% confidence and 2.575 is used for 99.5% confidence. Other values can be looked up in a table of the standard normal distribution (not used here).

A typical example where a one-sided test is **not** possible is described as follows. Suppose a bookseller claims to be faster in the delivery of books than a certain time period - say 2 months on the average. Suppose we order N books and we arrive at a mean delivery time $\overline{x} = 53$ days. Since $53 < 60$ and since the bookseller says this is always so, we might be inclined to test $\overline{x} < \mu$ − a one-sided test. This is wrong, because we do not know for sure that $\overline{x}$ will always be less than $\mu = 60$. Applying a one-sided test in this example gives a much higher chance that we will accept $\overline{x} \leq \mu$ than $\overline{x} = \mu$, and hence the bookseller's smooth talk has influenced our evaluation of their performance.

The above examples, though important, have one "unnatural" feature: one must have an idea on what to use as μ. In the last exercises this was quite natural but in other excercises this is not alltogether so. The next consequence of the first test of the mean does not need μ. In fact we present a method of estimating μ. This technique of determining confidence intervals for the population mean μ (based on a sample with parameters N, $\overline{x}$ and s) is one of the highlights of part 3 and is frequently used in reports.

3.3 Consequence of the first test of the mean: confidence intervals for the population mean μ

The central limit theorem as used in the previous section states that the sample averages $\overline{x}$ are normally distributed. This is why

$$Z = \frac{\overline{x} - \mu}{\frac{s}{\sqrt{N-1}}} \tag{3.1}$$

follows the standard normal distribution curve described earlier. Again from the previous section we know that 95% of the area under the standard normal distribution is obtained between the values -1.96 and 1.96 on the x-axis (for 99% this is so between the values -2.575 and 2.575). In other words in 95% of the cases the sample average $\overline{x}$ will be so that $-1.96 \le Z \le 1.96$ with Z as in formula (3.1). Putting it in another way,

$$-1.96 \le \frac{\overline{x} - \mu}{\frac{s}{\sqrt{N-1}}} \le 1.96 \tag{3.6}$$

is true in 95% of the cases. Formula (3.6) contains two algebraic inequalities which are equivalent to

$$\overline{x} - 1.96\frac{s}{\sqrt{N-1}} \le \mu \le \overline{x} + 1.96\frac{s}{\sqrt{N-1}} \tag{3.7}$$

In words, (3.7) states that it is 95% sure that μ, the population average (that is the unknown average of the studied characteristic in the complete universe, in our case a library, for example), lies in the interval

$$\left[\overline{x} - 1.96\frac{s}{\sqrt{N-1}}; \overline{x} + 1.96\frac{s}{\sqrt{N-1}}\right] \tag{3.8}$$

This can be interesting information about the global average of the characteristic under study. Of course, a 99% confidence interval is similarly given by

$$\left[\overline{x} - 2.575\frac{s}{\sqrt{N-1}}; \overline{x} + 2.575\frac{s}{\sqrt{N-1}}\right] \tag{3.9}$$

Note

As in the previous section, if $\overline{x}$ is a fraction we can use (3.3), hence

$$\frac{s}{\sqrt{N-1}} = \sqrt{\frac{\overline{x}(1-\overline{x})}{N-1}} \tag{3.10}$$

Exercises

1. A sample of 101 books in the library gives an average length of the reference list of 83.3 references (hence $\bar{x} = 83.3$). The standard deviation is $s = 12.15$. Determine a 99% confidence interval for the real average length of a reference list over all books in the library.

   Solution
   The confidence interval we want is given by (3.9):
   $$\left[83.3 - 2.575\frac{12.15}{\sqrt{100}}; 83.3 + 2.575\frac{12.15}{\sqrt{100}}\right] = [80.2; 86.4],$$
   so the real average μ is
   $$80.2 \leq \mu \leq 86.4,$$
   and we can be 99% sure of this.

2. A sample of 101 shelf metres (filled with books) gives an average number of books per metre $\bar{x} = 31.6$ with $s = 12.7$. Determine a 95% confidence interval for the library average number of books per metre.

   Solution
   Using (3.8), we obtain the interval $[29.1; 34.1]$.

3. (H. Voorbij, Royal Library, The Hague, Netherlands, oral communication). How many women with a university degree are members of the Royal Library? A sample of $N = 780$ from a total of 11 000 members in 1991 yields a fraction $\bar{x} = 0.072$.

   Solution
   (3.10) and (3.8) yield a 95% confidence interval
   $$[0.054; 0.090]$$
   for the expected fraction. Multiplying by 11 000 then gives us the expected number: we obtain a range between 594 and 990, a rather weak result. This is usually the case for small fractions: only larger groups can be studied effectively.

4. (H. Voorbij - see also exercise 3) Are there more people from outside the The Hague region who are members of the Royal Library, than from inside the region?

Solution

We draw a sample of $N = 300$ and find a fraction of $\bar{x} = 0.4$ from inside the region. With 95% certainty we then have a confidence interval of

$$[0.344; 0.456].$$

It is therefore more than 95% certain that we have more members from outside the region than from inside.

5. What is the average number of authors of mathematics books, given a sample with $N = 100$, $\bar{x} = 1.3$, $s = 1.48$?

Solution

It is 95% sure that the average is between 1.01 and 1.59.

6. What is the average delivery time of books from a bookseller? A sample yielded $N = 101$, $\bar{x} = 55.3$ days, $s = 15.73$.

Solution

It is 95% sure that the average delivery time for books from this bookseller is between 52.22 and 58.38 days.

7. We want to know the fraction of library users who agree with new opening hours. A sample yields $N = 123$, $\bar{x} = 0.63$.

Solution

A 99% confidence interval is given by $[0.52; 0.74]$. Hence, with more than 99% certainty, more than 50% approve the new opening hours.

8. Determine the fraction of circulations that contain the maximum number of books that are allowed to be borrowed in one time. A sample yields $N = 501$, $\bar{x} = 0.37$. A 95% confidence interval for the real fraction is $[0.33; 0.41]$.

9. In exercise 3 we mentioned the difficulty of measuring small fractions. Here is another example. We want to estimate the cumulative number of lost or damaged books, over a 5-year period (since the last check-up). A sample gives $N = 1\,000$, $\bar{x} = 0.025$ (i.e. 0.5% per year). A 95% confidence interval is $[0.015; 0.035]$ (which is a weak result). A sample size of $N = 10\,000$ is better and is manageable by using fast automated scanning techniques. In that case (still supposing $\bar{x} = 0.025$) we have the interval $[0.022; 0.028]$. If the library

contains 500 000 books then we estimate between 11 000 and 14 000 lost or damaged books over the last 5 years.

10. (H.Voorbij). We have a very large collection of catalogue cards. What fraction of these cards has already been entered in the automated database? A sample of only 500 cards yields $\overline{x} = 0.83$. We then are 95% sure that between 80% and 86% of the cards have been entered in the automated system.

11. (cf. exercise 3 in the previous section, but here the exercise is more "natural" since we do not have to "know" that $\mu = 12.4$).
    A sample ($N = 178$) in the database of female library users shows an average number of library visits per year of 14.7 with $s = 10.8$. Determine a 95% and 99% confidence interval for the real average number of library visits per year of female users. The solution is: $13.1 \leq \mu \leq 16.3, 95\%$ sure and $12.6 \leq \mu \leq 16.8, 99\%$ sure.

12. What is the fraction of borrowed books that are returned too late? A sample ($N = 2\,500$) yields $\overline{x} = 0.11$. We have

$$0.098 \leq \mu \leq 0.122, \ 95\% \text{ sure.}$$

13. Estimate the average number of library visitors reading at tables in the library. We sample ($N = 101$) and find $\overline{x} = 47$, $s = 12.8$.
    A 95% confidence interval is

$$[44.5; 49.5]$$

14. What is the fraction of library users who are willing to subscribe to an SDI-service (SDI = Selective Dissemination of Information, a current awareness service) of the library, knowing that there is a threshold of \$4 per month? A sample of 650 users gives $\overline{x} = 0.34$. A 95% confidence interval is

$$[0.304; 0.376]$$

15. Overlap studies are very important for all kinds of library activities. It is more and more necessary to have an idea of the overlap between your library and another one (or another group of libraries). The same is true for the overlap between databases. Overlap knowledge between libraries is useful in the inter-library services, for networking, union catalogues and so on. Overlap of library B with respect to library A can be defined as

$$O(B \mid A) = \frac{\#(A \cap B)}{\#A}. \tag{3.11}$$

The right-hand side of this equation is the quotient of the number of books that belong to both libraries and the number of books in library A. Hence, overlap is a fraction: it is the fraction of the books in A that also belong to B. Note that $O(B \mid A) \neq O(A \mid B)$. Since $O(B \mid A)$ is a fraction, all the results discussed above can be applied. For more on overlap, see Egghe and Rousseau (1990). Overlap can be depicted as in Fig. 3.3

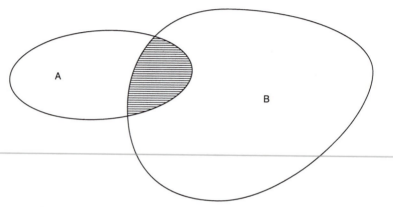

Fig. 3.3: Overlap of A with respect to B ($A \cap B$ with respect to B)
or overlap of B with respect to A ($A \cap B$ w.r.t. A)

Exercise
Determine the overlap of information science books of library B with respect to library A. A sample in the information science collection in A yields $\overline{x} = 0.64$, hence 64% of this sample also belongs to library B ($N = 781$). Then a 99% confidence interval for the real overlap is $[0.60; 0.68]$.

The next two tests for the mean deal with comparing the means of two data sets. This can be important for comparing the quality (or speed, price, and so on) of several services. Concrete examples will be given.

3.4 Second test for the mean: one sample but with two sets of measurements

The simple idea behind this case is to reduce the two measurements to one measurement by subtracting corresponding data. Then we apply the first test of Section 3.2.

Let us explain this with a concrete example.

Suppose we want to evaluate the speed of two OPACs in order to make a decision to use (or implement) the fastest one (the example could also be given for comparing any two retrieval systems, online, on disk, even manual systems). The method only works with a sample of size $N \geq 30$. For $N < 30$ there are corrections that can be executed manually but, as also mentioned in Section 3.2, when the calculations are done by a software package these are implemented automatically. To explain the method, we give all data but we take $N = 14$ here, for simplicity (but act as if $N \geq 30$: in practice we strongly advise making sure that $N \geq 30$ which will not be a problem in most real cases). We took 14 books of which we are sure they are present in both systems. The retrieval times in systems A and B, for searches performed by inexperienced library users, are as in Table 3.1 (in seconds)

Table 3.1: Retrieval times in two systems

Book	System A	System B	$B - A$
1	6	21	15
2	12	13	1
3	8	72	64
4	28	13	-15
5	13	40	27
6	12	51	39
7	48	34	-14
8	14	32	18
9	17	28	11
10	21	43	22
11	24	33	9
12	10	24	14
13	6	21	15
14	3	21	18

We calculate the difference of the two tables (symbolically $B - A$; one could also have calculated $A - B$, which would involve a change of sign). Note that the minus signs are important here (deleting them gives that, *a priori*, B is slower than A, no matter what the data are).

It is now clear that testing whether or not the average retrieval times of A are significantly different from the average retrieval times of B is the same as testing whether or not the average of the last column is significantly different from zero. Hence, we can perform the first test of the mean on the data of the last column, taking as population average $\mu = 0$. So the average and standard deviation of the last column must be determined, being $\bar{x}_{B-A} = 16$, $s_{B-A} = 19.2$. According to formula (3.2) we have

$$Z = \frac{\bar{x}_{B-A} - 0}{s_{B-A}}\sqrt{N-1}$$

$$Z = \frac{16}{19.2}\sqrt{13} = 3.00$$

Since $3.00 > 2.575$ we conclude that the average difference between the retrieval times in B and A is structurally different from zero (99% level). In other words, system B is slower than system A, a conclusion that we draw with more than 99% certainty. We again stress the fact that the above method is only correct for $N \geq 30$!

We present two more exercises.

Exercises

1. We fix one set of books ($N = 100$), available in two public libraries A and B. We check how many times these books were borrowed (on average) in both libraries in 1999. We give the summary statistics right away: the average difference (using $A - B$) is $\bar{x}_{A-B} = 0.3$ times and the standard deviation of the difference is $s_{A-B} = 5.4$. Is there a significant difference of use (in terms of circulations) of books in library A with respect to library B?

   Solution

   $$Z = \frac{0.3}{5.4}\sqrt{99} = 0.553$$

   Hence there is no significant difference.

   We note that in the above two examples we are restricted in our actions by requiring that the books are the same in both systems. It would be better to be allowed to check possibly different books in the two systems. The next exercise is even a clearer example of the restriction of this method. That is exactly why the third test for the mean (to follow in the next section) has been created.

2. We want to know whether or not there is a difference of delivery times of books between two booksellers. We order **the same** 80 books from both booksellers and denote the delivery times. For the column of differences we have

$\overline{x}_{A-B} = 12.7$ days with $s_{A-B} = 51.2$ days. Is this difference significant?

Solution

$$Z = \frac{12.7}{51.2}\sqrt{79} = 2.2 > 1.96$$

Hence, bookseller A is significantly slower (a 95% sure conclusion) but not 99% sure (2.2 < 2.575). Since we are dealing here with an important decision (which bookseller to use in future) perhaps we should postpone the decision, say for a year, and then perform a new test.

It is clear that the above exercise cannot be done in practice: we would have to order 80 books twice, which represents a loss of money because usually one does not order so many books twice. If you do, then perform this test; it is then more powerful than the next one (Section 3.5).

3. We study a fixed set of journal titles (157 titles but this number is not needed here), available in two libraries but delivered via the services of two different journal intermediaries. We measure the difference (in days) between the arrival dates of this year's issues between both libraries: we have a set of $N = 620$ issues that could be compared. We found $x_{A-B} = 3.5$ days with $s_{A-B} = 23$ days. Can we say that the deliveries for library A are significantly slower than those for library B?

Solution

$$Z = \frac{3.5}{23}\sqrt{619} = 3.786 > 2.575$$

Hence the service for A is significantly slower than the one for B.

As already said, in all these cases we need two identical sets on which we perform two measurements. The next test for the mean deals with the more realistic situation of testing two samples. This is another highlight of part 3, which can often be used in libraries.

3.5 Third test for the mean: two samples

As stated above, this is the most frequently used test for comparisons of two means. An example is the best way of explaining the method.

What we have now is two populations, say two booksellers A and B ("population" here means the unknown delivery capabilities of these booksellers). For each bookseller we check a number of ordered books (N_A for bookseller A and N_B for bookseller B) and note their delivery times. In each case we find an average ($\overline{x}_A$ and $\overline{x}_B$) and a standard deviation (s_A and s_B). The question is: is the difference between $\overline{x}_A$ and $\overline{x}_B$ large enough to conclude that the real difference in delivery capabilities of these booksellers is different from zero? The method says that we must calculate

$$Z = \frac{\overline{x}_B - \overline{x}_A}{\sqrt{\dfrac{s_A^2}{N_A - 1} + \dfrac{s_B^2}{N_B - 1}}} \tag{3.12}$$

and compare with the critical values 1.96 or 2.575. Let us fill in this example. Say we take 100 (different) ordered books at each bookseller: $N_A = N_B = 100$. N_A and N_B do not have to be equal, but it is best to keep them comparable in size of course so that A and B have comparable weights in this test. Suppose the delivery times are such that the summary statistics are (in days) : $\overline{x}_A = 95.9$, $s_A = 97.39$, $\overline{x}_B = 85.7$, $s_B = 114.4$. Then

$$Z = \frac{85.7 - 95.9}{\sqrt{\dfrac{(97.39)^2 + (114.4)^2}{99}}} = -0.676,$$

which is therefore not significant. We cannot conclude from these samples that bookseller B is faster than bookseller A. The reason is the high variances.

Exercises

1. As in the above example we could also compare delivery times for books coming from different countries. Note that here all books are necessarily different.

2. (Compare with exercise 1 in Section 3.2 and note the fact that the exercise here is far more natural!).

   We take a sample of 100 mathematics books and find that the average number of authors $\overline{x}_M = 1.3$, with standard deviation $s_M = 1.7$. For 150 chemistry books this is $\overline{x}_C = 1.8$ and $s_C = 2.1$. Are there significantly more authors per chemistry book than per mathematics book, on average?

   Solution

$$Z = \frac{1.8 - 1.3}{\sqrt{\dfrac{(1.7)^2}{99} + \dfrac{(2.1)^2}{149}}} = 2.062$$

Since 2.062 > 1.96 we can conclude that chemistry books have more co-authors than mathematics books (at the 95% level).

Note

When we deal with fractions (see Section 3.2), as in formula (3.3) we can replace s_A^2 by $\overline{x}_A(1 - \overline{x}_A)$ and the same for B. Hence, for fractions, formula (3.12) may be replaced by

$$Z = \frac{\overline{x}_B - \overline{x}_A}{\sqrt{\dfrac{\overline{x}_A(1 - \overline{x}_A)}{N_A - 1} + \dfrac{\overline{x}_B(1 - \overline{x}_B)}{N_B - 1}}}$$

3. Note here again the clear and natural question. In public library A we sampled ($N_A = 375$) 61% female users. In library B we sampled ($N_B = 405$), only 57%. Is this difference significant?

Solution

$$Z = \frac{0.57 - 0.61}{\sqrt{\dfrac{(0.61)(0.39)}{374} + \dfrac{(0.57)(0.43)}{404}}}$$

$$Z = -1.135$$

Since 1.135 < 1.96 we have a non-significant difference: the difference in female library users is not structural, at least on the basis of this sample.

4. In library A 27.5% of users are under 18 years old (following from a sample with size 286). In library B we found 30.4% (sample size of 307). Is the difference significant?

Solution

$Z = 0.778$, hence not significant.

5. We investigate the lending activities of two libraries for fiction books, and check how many times these books were borrowed (on average) in 1995. In library A we found $N_A = 570$ borrowings and in library B, $N_B = 595$ borrowings. We found $\overline{x}_A = 1.2$, $s_A = 1.1$ $\overline{x}_B = 1.0$, $s_B = 0.8$. Is the difference significant?

Solution

$Z = -3.54$, very significant.

6. A sample in village A amongst $N_A = 507$ inhabitants shows that 19% of them are members of the local public library. In village B we found ($N_B = 480$) 21%. Is this difference significant?

Solution

$Z = 0.784$, not significant enough.

7. A questionnaire on the measurement of the quality of certain library services shows that only 46% of the users are satisfied (281 forms were received). This score is considered too low and we work on the quality of the service (for example more staff, more friendly service and so on). After one year a new sample is performed (251 forms received) which finds that 58% of the users are satisfied. Is this a significant improvement?

Solution

$Z = 2.78$, significant (at least at the 1% level).

8. A librarian investigates the circulation activity (during a certain year) of the books in the library that are written in French. A sample of size $N_1 = 1\,075$ in the circulation data shows that these books constitute 11% of the total number of borrowings. The information is unwelcome since these books comprise 23% of the collection (this number is not needed further on in the calculations). The librarian decides to reorganise the library so that the French books are located in a more central place in the library. Next year, circulation data show that on a total of $N_2 = 981$ borrowings the French collection now represents 13% of the total number of borrowings. Has there been a significant improvement?

Solution

The answer is much shorter than the question:

$$Z = \frac{0.13 - 0.11}{\sqrt{\dfrac{(0.11)(0.89)}{1\,074} + \dfrac{(0.13)(0.87)}{980}}} = 1.39$$

hence not a significant result. The librarian's action has not really achieved anything.

9. A public library contains 115 fiction books by living national authors and 2 349 other fiction books by living authors from other countries.

The 115 books by national authors were circulated 695 times; the other fiction books were circulated 13 506 times. Is the fraction $\dfrac{115}{2\,464}$, (4.67%) of books by national authors significantly smaller that the corresponding fraction of circulations: $(\dfrac{695}{14\,201}$ or 4.89%)? In other words, are national authors read more?

Solution

$$Z = \frac{0.0489 - 0.0467}{\sqrt{\dfrac{0.0467 \times 0.9533}{2\,464} + \dfrac{0.0489 \times 0.9511}{14\,201}}}$$

$$Z = 0.015$$

evidently not significant.

Now we will deal with the important problem of sample sizes.

3.6 Sample sizes

At last we come on to the topic of sample sizes. The method can be used for one sample (Sections 3.2 and 3.3 on the data itself), on the data of the differences between the two measurements (Section 3.4) or for two samples (Section 3.5) where we apply the present theory twice.

We therefore suppose we have the same situation as in Sections 3.2 or 3.3. The problem we want to study here is: how large must the sample size N be in order to obtain confidence intervals with given specifications? Note that the cases we refer to consist already of samples with a mean and a standard deviation. Hence, the problem we have to consider is that of a possible enlargement of the sample in order to satisfy the required specifications.

3.6.1 Rough argument

The most important and interesting problem is to keep the confidence intervals of Section 3.3 as small as possible. In some exercises we noted that results were rather weak because the length of the confidence intervals was too large. What is the length of a confidence interval? Let us look at the 95% confidence interval (3.8). Making a drawing of this on the x-axis yields Fig. 3.4.

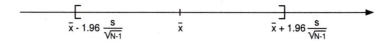

Fig. 3.4: A 95% confidence interval

From this graph it is clear that the length of a 95% confidence interval is given by

$$2 \times 1.96 \frac{s}{\sqrt{N-1}} \tag{3.13}$$

Suppose we require this length to be smaller than a positive number α, chosen by us. This requirement leads to the following algebraic inequality:

$$2 \times 1.96 \frac{s}{\sqrt{N-1}} \leq \alpha \tag{3.14}$$

This yields (we omit the calculation):

$$N \geq \frac{15.37 s^2}{\alpha^2} + 1 \tag{3.15}$$

For 99% confidence intervals we have to replace 1.96 by 2.575 (cf. formula (3.9)) in Fig. 3.4. Then the inequality

$$N \geq \frac{26.52 s^2}{\alpha^2} + 1 \tag{3.16}$$

replaces (3.15).

3.6.2   Logical correction and refinement

The above derivation is correct, but there is a logical inconsistency. We want to determine the sample size, which is achieved, (cf. formulae (3.15) and (3.16)) but in the formulae we see the appearance of s^2, which is in fact the variance of a sample that we are about to determine! The solution lies in so-called "two-stage sampling", which goes as follows:

- Draw a preliminary sample (rather small but of size at least 30) in order to get an idea of $\bar{x}$ and s. The size of this preliminary sample is not determined. Its only goal is to give reasonable estimates for $\bar{x}$ and s.

- Calculate (3.15) or (3.16) with this s and see what minimum value of N is required.

- The preliminary sample is not lost work: we simply complete the first sample in order to arrive at this minimum sample size level.

Of course, in this larger sample $\bar{x}$ and s^2 can change a bit. Possibly a third sample is needed but we will not go in to this: for us the two-stage sample suffices.

The fact that we also get an idea of the value of $\bar{x}$ via this preliminary sample allows us to improve formulae (3.15) and (3.16) by replacing α by a value that is more appropriate with $\bar{x}$. Indeed, α clearly depends on $\bar{x}$. It makes no sense to require $\alpha = 5$ if the characteristic we are dealing with is: number of authors per book. Here a value of 0.2 or 0.3 is more appropriate. The latter values, in turn, are not very reasonable when dealing with the number of books per metre of shelf.

It is therefore best to link α to $\bar{x}$ as follows: let

$$\alpha = \theta\bar{x} \tag{3.17}$$

That is, we require the total length of the confidence interval to be a function of $\bar{x}$ (say $0.2\,\bar{x}$ or any other reasonable value). Using this formalism we have for formulae (3.15) and (3.16):

$$N \geq \frac{15.37 s^2}{\theta^2\bar{x}^2} + 1 \qquad \text{(95\% confidence interval)} \tag{3.18}$$

and

$$N \geq \frac{26.52 s^2}{\theta^2\bar{x}^2} + 1 \qquad \text{(99\% confidence interval)} \tag{3.19}$$

If we are working with fractions, then (3.3) gives $s^2 = \bar{x}(1 - \bar{x})$. Hence

$$\frac{s^2}{\theta^2\bar{x}^2} = \frac{\bar{x}(1 - \bar{x})}{\theta^2\bar{x}^2}$$

$$= \frac{1 - \bar{x}}{\theta^2\bar{x}}$$

Putting this into (3.18) and (3.19) gives, **for fractions**:

$$N \geq \frac{15.37(1 - \bar{x})}{\theta^2\bar{x}} + 1 \tag{3.20}$$

and

$$N \geq \frac{26.52(1 - \bar{x})}{\theta^2\bar{x}} + 1 \tag{3.21}$$

Many exercises now follow. Note also that all the previous exercises in part 3 can be used to determine sample sizes in order to reduce confidence intervals.

Example

In exercise 5 in Section 3.3 we found the 95% confidence interval $[1.01; 1.59]$ for the average number of authors of mathematics books. We use this sample as our preliminary sample. Suppose we require $\alpha = 0.5$ (instead of 0.58 now) then we require, using formula (3.15) and the data of exercise 5 in Section 3.3:

$$N \geq \frac{(15.37)(2.2)}{(0.5)(0.5)} + 1 = 136.26$$

Hence we take $N \geq 137$. If we require that the total length of the 95% confidence interval is less than 0.2 we then have

$$N \geq \frac{(15.37)(2.2)}{(0.2)(0.2)} + 1 = 846.35$$

Hence a minimum sample of $N \geq 847$ is now needed.

Note

With $N \geq 847$ the confidence interval has a length of 0.2, that is if $\bar{x}$ and s of this enlarged sample remain the same. Small changes might occur, so that 0.2 might not be reached at once. Another correction (increase of N) might be necessary, but we do not go into this. If $\bar{x}$ and s have not changed we therefore now have a confidence interval $[1.2; 1.4]$ which is 95% accurate.

Exercises

1. We wish to estimate the average number of authors of chemistry articles. A preliminary sample yields $\bar{x} = 3.9$, $s^2 = 3.5$. We require $\alpha = 0.2\bar{x}$ (meaning that the confidence interval must have a length not larger than one-fifth of $\bar{x}$).

   Solution
   (3.18) for a 95% confidence interval gives, since $\theta = 0.2$,

   $$N \geq \frac{(15.37)(3.5)}{(0.2)^2(3.9)^2} + 1 = 89.4$$

   Hence $N \geq 90$ necessarily. Formula (3.19) for a 99% confidence interval gives

   $$N \geq \frac{(26.52)(3.5)}{(0.2)^2(3.9)^2} + 1 = 153.6$$

   Hence $N \geq 154$ is required.

   If, with these enlarged samples, $\bar{x}$ and s have not changed, we now have a confidence interval ($\theta = 0.2$):

   $$[3.9 - 0.39; 3.9 + 0.39] = [3.51; 4.29]$$

   (95% or 99% sure, according to the two cases above).

2. We want to know a bookseller's average delivery time (in days). We want a 99% sure conclusion and an interval length of maximum 10% of the estimated average delivery time (so $\theta = 0.1$). A preliminary sample yields $\bar{x} = 55.3$ days and $s^2 = 247.3$.

   Solution
   (3.19) yields

   $$N \geq \frac{(26.52)(247.3)}{(0.1)^2(55.3)^2} + 1 = 215.5,$$

   hence $N \geq 216$ is necessary. For 95% we have $N \geq 126$ (check this). We leave it to the reader to write down the obtained confidence interval.

3. (cf. exercise 7 in Section 3.3). We use this sample as our preliminary sample. We now require $\theta = 0.2$ (meaning that there is 10% leeway to the left and right of $\bar{x}$).

Solution

For a 95% confidence interval

$$N \geq \frac{(15.37)(0.37)}{(0.2)^2(0.63)} + 1 = 225.7,$$

according to formula (3.20) (fractions).

Hence $N \geq 226$ suffices. Of course, as is clear from the formulae, θ^2 is in the denominator. Hence, if we require θ to be very small, N increases steadily. For example, changing $\theta = 0.2$ to $\theta = 0.1$ now gives $N \geq 904$ for formula (3.20) (check this!).

4. (cf. exercise 8 in Section 3.3). Again we use this sample as a preliminary sample. We require $\theta = 0.2$ and a 99% sure conclusion. We have, by (3.21),

$$N \geq \frac{(26.52)(0.63)}{(0.2)^2(0.37)} = 1129.9,$$

hence $N \geq 1130$.

5. We study further exercise 9 in Section 3.3 and use the sample there as our preliminary sample. We again require $\theta = 0.2$ and a 95% sure conclusion. Formula (3.20) yields

$$N \geq \frac{(15.37)(0.975)}{(0.2)^2(0.025)} + 1 = 14\,986.8$$

Hence we take a sample of $N = 14\,987$. Of course, as always, the preliminary sample can still be used (size $= 1\,000$); we just have to add $13\,987$ more checks to it. Since this number is much larger than $1\,000$ we might end up with a different $\bar{x}$ (in fact this can happen any time N is increased). Suppose we have now $\bar{x} = 0.023$. Then, 95% certainly, the fraction of lost books lies in ($\theta = 0.2$):

$$[0.023 - 0.0023; 0.023 + 0.0023] = [0.0207; 0.0253],$$

hence between 2.1% and 2.5%. For a library of $500\,000$ books this gives an estimate of the number of lost books between $0.0207 \times 500\,000 = 10\,350$ and $0.0253 \times 500\,000 = 12\,650$.

Checking about $15\,000$ books is not as unrealistic as it might seem: using a portable bar code scanner, for instance, this is a feasible enterprise.

This exercise dealt with lost books over a 5-year period. Indeed, it is best **not** to perform such an exercise on a yearly basis since lost books might show up in the coming months.

6. A variant of the above exercise is as follows. A sample of 100 books drawn from a section in the library indicates that 3% of the books are lost. There are 6 000 books in this section. We want to know the number of lost books with an error of at most 40 books with 95% certainty. How large is the sample we have to use?

Solution

We use (3.15) with $\alpha = \dfrac{40}{6\,000} = \dfrac{1}{150}$ and $s^2 = \bar{x}(1 - \bar{x}) = 0.03 \times 0.97 = 0.0291$:

$$N \geq \frac{15.37 \times 0.0291}{\left(\dfrac{1}{150}\right)^2} + 1 = 10\,064.5.$$

Hence we must check 10 065 books.

7. (cf. exercise 10 in Section 3.3). We use this sample as our preliminary sample. We are very strict now: we require $\theta = 0.1$ (meaning that to the left and right of $\bar{x}$ only 5% of $\bar{x}$ is allowed as leeway). For a 95% confidence interval we have

$$N \geq \frac{(15.37)(0.17)}{(0.1)^2(0.83)} + 1 = 315.8,$$

hence $N \geq 316$.

8. Overlap (cf. exercise 15 in Section 3.3). We again use this sample as our preliminary sample. We require $\theta = 0.1$. We find $N \geq 866$ (check this). Suppose the new $\bar{x}$ is changed to 0.61. Then $O(B \mid A)$ is 95% sure between the values $0.61 - \dfrac{0.61}{20} = 0.58$ and $0.61 + \dfrac{0.61}{20} = 0.64$, hence an overlap between 58% and 64%.

For more on two-stage sampling in a library context, see Miller and Sorum (1977).

3.7 Confidence intervals and sample sizes for multinomial fractions

3.7.1 Introduction

In Section 3.2 we discussed the issue of fractions. There we limited the discussion to binomial fractions, − fractions where we are interested in one part of a population and do not subdivide the other part, giving a situation such as that depicted in Fig. 3.5.

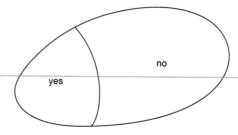

Fig.3.5: Binomial fractions

Examples are yes−no situations (as answer to a question), 0−1 situations, male−female distributions, and so on. A concrete example of this is estimating the fraction of female library users. Any sample gives a score 1 to a female and 0 to a male. The average $\bar{x}$ is then the sampled fraction of female users of the library. Of course we might be interested in more detailed information, such as the fraction of female users whose ages are between 20 (inclusive) and 30 (not inclusive). If we want to interpret this as a binomial situation we give a score 1 to female users with age in the half-open interval $[20, 30[$ and a 0 to any other user (all males and all females whose age is not in the interval $[20, 30[$).

All these cases lead to confidence intervals for the population mean (fraction) μ of the form (cf. formulae (3.8), (3.9) and (3.10)):

$$\left[\bar{x} - 1.96\sqrt{\frac{\bar{x}(1-\bar{x})}{N-1}}, \bar{x} + 1.96\sqrt{\frac{\bar{x}(1-\bar{x})}{N-1}}\right] \quad \text{(95\% confidence interval)} \quad (3.22)$$

and

$$\left[\overline{x} - 2.575\sqrt{\frac{\overline{x}(1-\overline{x})}{N-1}}, \overline{x} + 2.575\sqrt{\frac{\overline{x}(1-\overline{x})}{N-1}}\right] \qquad (99\% \text{ confidence interval}) \quad (3.23)$$

Of course, the last example is not very natural: if we are interested in the fraction of female users aged between 20 and 30, then we are normally also interested in the fraction of female users in other age categories (and the same for the male users). In other words we are interested in multinomial fractions, symbolically depicted as in Fig. 3.6.

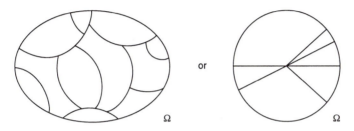

or

Ω

Ω

Fig. 3.6: Multinomial fractions

Estimating multinomial fractions (using confidence intervals) is a very important problem, and examples abound:

- The above example: fractions of library users, subdivided according to gender and a number of age classes.

- The fractions of library books with n authors ($n = 0, 1, 2, 3, \ldots$), possibly further subdivided according to language and age of the book and the fact that the book is or is not in the automated catalogue of the library.

- Fractions of employees in different salary scales.

- Fractions of people with different blood groups.

- Estimating the results of political parties at the next election.

- (cf. H. Voorbij, exercise 10 in Section 3.3 — now interpreted in a multinomial way). The fractions of books with catalogue cards that are in the automated catalogue or not, are written in certain languages and have been published in different time periods.

- (cf. H. Voorbij, exercise 3 in Section 3.3 — multinomial version). Determine year-by-year fractions of women with an academic degree registered in the library from 1985 on. Analogously, determine the fraction of pupils of age 12, 13,..., 18, who are library members.

It was in fact H. Voorbij who posed questions like this to one of the present authors (Egghe). What seemed to be a simple extension of the well-known binomial case turned out to be a problem with only a partial solution, in the sense that quite often the sample sizes are not controllable any more without reducing the number of classes (thereby increasing the lowest fractions). We refer the reader to Johnson and Wichern (1988), Chapter 5 and especially to p.188−190 about the so-called Bonferroni method, adopted here, which seems to give relatively good results (see also Egghe and Veraverbeke (1995) for a comparison of different methods and for discussions on further applications).

It must be stressed that the above - mentioned problem is

- very important, inside and outside our field

- hardly covered in the scientific literature in books and certainly not in books on library and related sciences

- easy to apply, but sometimes leads to large sample sizes.

The intuitive reason for the large sample sizes or, equivalently, low confidence of the confidence intervals obtained, is that for every fraction **separately** we have the well-known confidence intervals, say with a confidence of 95%, but their joint confidence (a conclusion about all the fractions) is of course much smaller. Compare with throwing a dice: predicting two throws gives a probability of $\frac{1}{36}$ as compared with predicting one score, which has a probability of $\frac{1}{6}$ − the problem here is even more complicated since the fractions are not independent (as is the case with the throwing of a dice): indeed, the total sum of all the fractions is 1.

Many persons make mistakes about this: they predict multinomial fractions by using binomial confidence intervals. Especially in poll ratings (elections) people make too many optimistic predictions (too optimistic in the sense that they attribute too high a probability to their conclusions).

3.7.2 The correct method for determining multinomial confidence intervals

We refer to Johnson and Wichern (1988) or Egghe and Veraverbeke (1995) for details and explanations. Here we only give the practical results.

Suppose we have k classes, hence k fractions to estimate. Suppose we have drawn a sample of size N in the total population (more on N later). This yields an estimate of the k fractions (of elements belonging to the k classes). Denote these k sampled fractions by $\overline{x}_1, \ldots, \overline{x}_k$. Note that if $k = 2$ we are back to the binomial case and to formulae (3.22) and (3.23) for the 95% and 99% confidence intervals of, for example $\overline{x}_1$; the confidence intervals for $\overline{x}_2$ follow immediately since now

$$\overline{x}_2 = 1 - \overline{x}_1 \tag{3.24}$$

In general, of course

$$\sum_{i=1}^{k} \overline{x}_i = 1 \tag{3.25}$$

We can present the following correct 95% confidence intervals for the k fractions $\overline{x}_1, \ldots, \overline{x}_k$:

$$\left[\overline{x}_i - a_k \sqrt{\frac{\overline{x}_i(1 - \overline{x}_i)}{N - 1}}, \overline{x}_i + a_k \sqrt{\frac{\overline{x}_i(1 - \overline{x}_i)}{N - 1}} \right] \tag{3.26}$$

$(i = 1, \ldots, k)$ where the a_k are given by Table 3.2.

Table 3.2: Values of a_k (95% confidence case)

k	3	4	5	6	7	8	9	10	11
a_k	2.39	2.50	2.57	2.64	2.69	2.73	2.77	2.81	2.84
k	12	13	14	15	16	17	18	19	20
a_k	2.86	2.89	2.91	2.93	2.95	2.97	2.99	3.01	3.03

It is therefore very simple: just replace 1.96 by the corresponding value of a_k (depending on the number of classes: the higher k, the higher a_k). We only consider here $k \leq 20$ and hence higher values of k are not presented. In fact he amount of work (i.e. sample size) required in order to arrive at acceptable confidence intervals becomes unreasonable when k is high. The higher the value of k, the more small fractions occur, and we know already from Section 3.3 that, even in the binomial case, estimating small fractions is difficult and this is even more so here because the values a_k are larger than 1.96.

The same can be done for 99% confidence intervals for the k fractions $\overline{x}_1, \ldots, \overline{x}_k$:

$$\left[\overline{x}_i - b_k \sqrt{\frac{\overline{x}_i(1 - \overline{x}_i)}{N - 1}}, \overline{x}_i + b_k \sqrt{\frac{\overline{x}_i(1 - \overline{x}_i)}{N - 1}} \right] \tag{3.27}$$

$(i = 1, \ldots, k)$ where the b_k are given by Table 3.3.

Table 3.3: Values of b_k (99% confidence case)

k	3	4	5	6	7	8	9	10	11
b_k	2.94	3.03	3.09	3.15	3.19	3.23	3.27	3.29	3.32
k	12	13	14	15	16	17	18	19	20
b_k	3.35	3.37	3.39	3.40	3.42	3.44	3.46	3.47	3.48

Example

We have checked the fractions of the books in the library with 1, 2, 3, 4 or more authors. A sample of size $N = 1\,176$ yielded the data shown in Table 3.4.

Table 3.4: Data on fractions of books with 1, 2, 3, 4 or more authors

Number of authors	i	N_i	$\overline{x}_i$
1	1	458	0.39
2	2	412	0.35
3	3	212	0.18
4 or more	4	94	0.08
		$N = 1\,176$	

We now calculate the four confidence intervals (95% confidence), using a_4 of Table 3.2. For $\overline{x}_1$ this is

$$\left[\overline{x}_1 - a_4 \sqrt{\frac{\overline{x}_1(1 - \overline{x}_1)}{N - 1}}, \overline{x}_1 + a_4 \sqrt{\frac{\overline{x}_1(1 - \overline{x}_1)}{N - 1}} \right]$$

$$= \left[0.39 - 2.5 \sqrt{\frac{(0.39)(0.61)}{1\,175}}, 0.39 + 2.5 \sqrt{\frac{(0.39)(0.61)}{1\,175}} \right]$$

$$= [0.354; 0.426]$$

So the real population (library) fraction of books with one author is between 0.354 and 0.426, with 95% certainty. This result must be expressed in conjunction with the three other confidence intervals: for $\overline{x}_2 : [0.315; 0.385]$, for $\overline{x}_3 : [0.152; 0.208]$ and for $\overline{x}_4 : [0.060; 0.100]$. These are reasonable results.

Remark

The value of $a_4 \cong 2.5$ for 95% confidence intervals for $k = 4$ is about the same as the value 2.575 yielding 99% confidence in the binomial ($k = 2$) case!

Note a sample size of $N = 300$ (keeping the same fractions $\overline{x}_1, \overline{x}_2, \overline{x}_3, \overline{x}_4$) would yield much worse intervals for $\overline{x}_1, \overline{x}_2, \overline{x}_3, \overline{x}_4$: $[0.320; 0.460]$, $[0.246; 0.454]$, $[0.097; 0.263]$, $[0.021; 0.139]$ (verify). Also note again that, the smaller $\overline{x}_i$ is (here $\overline{x}_4$) the worse the result.

The reader is advised to make the same calculations for 99% confidence intervals, using $b_4 = 3.03$ of Table 3.3.

We now present an exercise with 16 classes from which it will be clear that either N must be increased considerably, or one must join together the (smallest) classes in order to reduce k, or both!

Exercise

What are the fractions of library users as divided by gender (2 classes) and 8 age classes as follows:

1:	≤ 10 years;	2:	11−20 years
3:	21−30 years;	4:	31−40 years,
5:	41−50 years;	6:	51−60 years,
7:	61−70 years;	8:	>70 years.

A sample of size $N = 324$ yielded the following data ($2 \times 8 = 16$ classes): see Table 3.5.

Table 3.5: Data on library users divided according to gender and age.

	1	2	3	4	5	6	7	8	Total
M	11	21	39	35	22	20	10	10	168
F	10	19	35	40	24	15	7	6	156
Total	21	40	74	75	46	35	17	16	$N = 324$

These numbers, divided by N yield the fractions $\overline{x}_1, \ldots, \overline{x}_{16}$, see Table 3.6.

Table 3.6: Fractions of library users, based on Table 3.5

	1	2	3	4	5	6	7	8
M	0.034	0.065	0.120	0.108	0.068	0.061	0.031	0.031
F	0.031	0.059	0.108	0.123	0.074	0.046	0.022	0.019

95% confidence intervals need the number a_{16} of Table 3.2: $a_{16} = 2.95$. For $\overline{x}_1$ we have

$$\left[0.034 - 2.95\sqrt{\frac{(0.034)(0.966)}{323}}, 0.034 + 2.95\sqrt{\frac{(0.034)(0.966)}{323}} \right]$$
$$= [0.004; 0.064]$$

This is a weak result. Verify that for cell $(F, 4)$ we have $[0, 069; 0, 177]$. Check the confidence intervals when N is increased to $3\,240$.

Finally, we note another example for which it is not easy to apply the above method. Suppose one decides to reward authors according to how often their books are borrowed in a country's public library system. Of course, it is too much work to keep track of all lending activities. So one decides to pick a few libraries every year which must then collect all lending data. On the basis of these data we want to determine the amount of money that will be given to each author as their reward.

It is clear from what we have said above that the vast number of authors represents a severe difficulty in the sense that the requested sample sizes must be very large. In practice, therefore, we think that this method does not work. We can only hope for automatic systems that can register every transaction.

3.7.3 Sample sizes for multinomial confidence intervals

As in the binomial case, we can produce minimum sample sizes in order to require a maximum length $\theta \overline{x}_i$ for **all** the confidence intervals. As in Subsection 3.6.2 we will work with a $\overline{x}_i$-related length $\theta \overline{x}_i$, for the ith interval ($i = 1 \ldots, k$) (cf. formula 3.17). For 95% confidence, we hence have the requirement (cf. formula (3.26)).

$$2a_k \sqrt{\frac{\overline{x}_i(1 - \overline{x}_i)}{N - 1}} \leq \theta \overline{x}_i$$

for **every** $i = 1, \ldots, k$. This gives the requirement

$$N \geq \frac{4a_k^2(1 - \overline{x}_i)}{\theta^2 \overline{x}_i} + 1 \tag{3.28}$$

for **every** $i = 1, \ldots, k$. For 99% confidence, just replace a_k by b_k.

Again, as in the binomial case, these formulae require a preliminary sample.

Exercises

1. For 95% confidence, $k = 4$, data as in the example, $\theta = 0.1$. So we require every confidence interval to have a length of 10% of the value of $\overline{x}_i$. We find

$$N \geq \frac{4(2.5)^2(1 - \overline{x}_i)}{(0.1)^2 \overline{x}_i} + 1$$

The largest of these four numbers is for the smallest fraction ($\overline{x}_4$), as can easily be proved. Hence

$$N \geq \frac{4(2.5)^2(1 - \overline{x}_4)}{(0.1)^2 \overline{x}_4} + 1 = 28\,751$$

which is a large number. A solution exists in dropping the classes with the smallest fractions: we combine $\overline{x}_3$ and $\overline{x}_4$ to make $\overline{x}_3' = 0.18 + 0.08 = 0.26$ and keep $\overline{x}_1$ and $\overline{x}_2$. Now $k = 3$ and the smallest fraction is $\overline{x}_3' = 0.26$. Formula (3.28) now yields (for $\theta = 0.1$)

$$N \geq \frac{4(2.39)^2(0.74)}{(0.1)^2(0.26)} + 1 = 6\,504$$

a much better result.

2. We have the following preliminary data on the number of books in our library published in America, Europe and the rest of the world: $N = 3\,000$ from which 51% from America, 37% from Europe and 12% for the rest. Hence $\overline{x}_1 = 0.51$, $\overline{x}_2 = 0,37$, $\overline{x}_3 = 0.12$. Make 95% confidence intervals so that the deviation is not more than 20% of the $\overline{x}_i$.

Solution

Formula (3.28) yields

$$N \geq \frac{4(2.39)^2(0.88)}{(0.2)^2(0.12)} + 1 = 4\,190$$

So we add another $1\,190$ books to our sample. Suppose the $\overline{x}_1$, $\overline{x}_2$, $\overline{x}_3$ fractions remained the same. Then we have the following 95% confidence intervals:

For $\overline{x}_1$:

$$\left[0.51 - 2.39\sqrt{\frac{(0.51)(0.49)}{4\,189}}; 0.51 + 2.39\sqrt{\frac{(0.51)(0.49)}{4\,189}} \right] = [0.492; 0.528]$$

For $\overline{x}_2$: $[0.352; 0.388]$
For $\overline{x}_3$: $[0.108; 0.132]$

Hence the library's total fraction of books from America is between 49.2% and 52.8%, the fraction of books from Europe is between 35.2% and 38.8% and the rest between 10.8% and 13.2%. Note that the confidence intervals for the higher fractions are (relatively) the best and their length is even smaller than $\theta\overline{x}_i$ ($i = 1, 2$) since the requirement on N is the strongest for $\overline{x}_3$.

This example shows that reasonable results are possible if we limit the number of classes and exclude small fractions (again by reducing the number of classes), and if we are prepared to live with somewhat higher sample sizes N.

General remark

In this section we dealt with confidence intervals for multinomial fractions $\overline{x}_1, \ldots, \overline{x}_k$. It is clear that the events $1, \ldots, k$ are not independent since, by (3.25),

$$\sum_{i=1}^{k} \overline{x}_i = 1.$$

Let us consider k independent events (fractions or not) for which k confidence intervals are known (say all on the 95% level). Then we can make a joint statement for all

94

these events at the level $(0.95)^k$. This is a consequence of the independence of these events.

Examples

1. Suppose we found a 95% confidence interval of $[0.3; 0.4]$ for the fraction of yellow books in mathematics and a 95% confidence interval of $[3 \text{ cm}; 3.5 \text{ cm}]$ for the average thickness of books in mathematics. The "joint statement" (that both confidence intervals apply) is true at a level of $(0.95)^2 = 0.9025$ (about 90%), supposing independence.

   In general, when we have k, $100(1 - \alpha_i)\%$ confidence intervals $(i = 1, \ldots, k)$ of independent events, then the joint statement is valid at a level of

   $$100 \prod_{i=1}^{k} (1 - \alpha_i)\%$$

2. We suppose that the delivery times for books from a supplier is independent of the delivery times for interlibrary ordered books. Suppose we found a 95% confidence interval in the first case and a 99% confidence interval in the second case. The "joint" conclusion (that we have both confidence intervals) is sure for

   $$100 \times 0.95 \times 0.99\% = 94.05\%$$

3.8   Epilogue: test for the quality of a regression line of a scatterplot — the correlation coefficient

In Section 2.1.4 we discussed "clouds of points" and the best-fitting straight line, called the regression line. In Section 2.2.5 we also presented explicit calculations of the regression line, as follows. Let

$$\{(x_1, y_1), (x_2, y_2), \ldots, (x_N, y_N)\}$$

be the set of points. Then its regression line has the equation

$$y = a + bx,$$

where

$$b = \frac{\dfrac{1}{N}\displaystyle\sum_{i=1}^{N} x_i y_i - \overline{x}\cdot\overline{y}}{\dfrac{1}{N}\displaystyle\sum_{i=1}^{N} x_i^2 - \overline{x}^2}$$

$$a = \overline{y} - b\overline{x}$$

(cf. formulae (2.15) and (2.16)).

These calculations are always possible, for any set of points. It is clear that not all relations between the x-variable and the y-variable are linear, but a regression line can also be calculated in these cases.

We need therefore a measure of the quality of the regression line or, stated more exactly, of the quality of the fit of the regression line to the scatterplot. Such a measure exists and is called the correlation coefficient (or Pearson's correlation coefficient). Its formula is

$$r = \frac{\dfrac{1}{N}\displaystyle\sum_{i=1}^{N} x_i y_i - \overline{x}\cdot\overline{y}}{s_x s_y} \tag{3.29}$$

(s_x are s_y the standard deviations of the x-values and the y-values respectively). Hence

$$r = \frac{b s_x}{s_y} \tag{3.30}$$

or, explicitly,

$$r = \frac{\dfrac{1}{N}\displaystyle\sum_{i=1}^{N} x_i y_i - \overline{x}\cdot\overline{y}}{\sqrt{\left(\dfrac{1}{N}\displaystyle\sum_{i=1}^{N} x_i^2 - \overline{x}^2\right)\left(\dfrac{1}{N}\displaystyle\sum_{i=1}^{N} y_i^2 - \overline{y}^2\right)}} \tag{3.31}$$

This measure is calculated automatically when one uses a statistical software package or a statistical pocket calculator. For a good understanding, we present an explicit calculation of r in the case of exercise 4 in Section 2.1.4. We refer to Table 2.4. Using this table it is easy to find r:

$$r = \frac{\dfrac{1}{10}146.33 - (2.515)(5.27)}{\sqrt{\left(\dfrac{1}{10}67.39 - (2.515)^2\right)\left(\dfrac{1}{10}326.19 - (5.27)^2\right)}}$$

$$r = 0.97.$$

Note that always

$$-1 \leq r \leq 1$$

and that r and b have the same sign (hence $r < 0$ for a decreasing regression line and $r > 0$ for an increasing one) and that, the closer r is to -1 or to 1, the better is the linear fit. These facts are clearly depicted in Fig. 3.7.

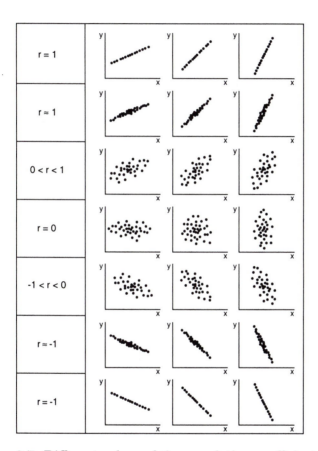

Fig. 3.7: Different values of the correlation coefficient r

Here we found $r = 0.97$, hence close to 1. However, this is not enough to conclude that r is sufficiently close to 1. In fact, when N is high even lower values of r are also sufficiently close to 1. What is the criterion?

Depending on N we present the following Table 3.7 with critical values of r: if r

is above this value then the linear relationship is accepted at the 95% or 99% level (i.e. we only have 5% or 1% respectively chance of being wrong in this — compare with the test for the mean in Sections 3.1 and 3.2). We only present the results for N up to 100 (values not given can be calculated via linear interpolation); more detailed tables are available in the statistical literature (again, when using a statistical software package, we do not have to worry about this).

Table 3.7: Table of critical values for r

N	95%	99%	N	95%	99%
5	0.878	0.959	17	0.482	0.606
6	0.811	0.917	18	0.468	0.590
7	0.754	0.875	19	0.456	0.575
8	0.707	0.834	20	0.444	0.561
9	0.666	0.798	25	0.396	0.505
10	0.632	0.765	30	0.361	0.463
11	0.602	0.735	35	0.334	0.430
12	0.576	0.708	40	0.312	0.402
13	0.553	0.684	50	0.279	0.361
14	0.532	0.661	60	0.254	0.330
15	0.514	0.641	80	0.220	0.286
16	0.497	0.623	100	0.196	0.256

For negative values of r change the signs in the above table and check whether r is below these values for significance (or simply use $-r$ in Table 3.7).

In the exercise above, $r = 0.97$, $N = 10$, hence r is certainly high enough. We can conclude with more than 99% certainty that the calculated regression line fits the scatterplot very well.

The above table can also be used for values of N above 100. Say $N = 123$ and we have $r = 0.26$. Note that, the higher the value of N, the lower the critical values of r. Now $0.26 > 0.256 > 0.196$, the critical values of r for $N = 100$. Since the critical values of r for $N = 123$ are even lower, we conclude that, even with 99% certainty, the regression line is well-fitting.

The reader is invited to calculate the following results using the exercises from Section 2.1.4.

98

1. Exercise 1 with regression line

$$y = 313.6 + 77.2t$$

   $r = 0.95$, high enough even at the 99% level.

2. Exercise 2 with regression line

$$y = 1.57 - 0.13t$$

   $r = -0.95$, low enough even at the 99% level.

3. Exercise 3 with regression line

$$y = 97.4 + 2.7t$$

   $r = 0.997$, again very high.

4. Exercise 4 with regression line

$$y = -3.10 + 3.33x$$

   $r = 0.97$, very high.

5. Exercise 5 with regression line

$$y = 334.2 + 0.34x$$

   $r = 0.39$, $N = 10$. Hence we cannot possibly accept that the above regression line fits the data, and this relationship between incoming and outgoing inter-library requests is not proved. In fact, the authors would be surprised to find any relationship at all between these two variables!

6. Exercise 6 with regression line

$$N(m) = 0.18 + 0.47m$$

   $r = 0.99$, very high.

7. Exercise 7 with regression line

$$N(m) = 0.45 + 0.55m$$

   $r = 0.815$, accepted with 95% of confidence but not with 99%.

8. Exercise 8 with regression line

$$y = 29.3 + 5.25x$$

$r = 0.939$; so linearity is accepted at any reasonable level.

9. Exercise 9 with regression line

$$\text{Journal budget} = 254 + 31 \times \text{ year}$$

$r = 0.981$, again very high.

10. Exercise 10 with regression line

$$\text{Number of misplaced books} = 21.8 + 0.14 \times \text{ height}$$

$r = 0.556$. Here we cannot conclude that there is a linear relationship.

11. Exercise 11 with regression line

$$\text{Number of users} = 862.1 - 40.37 \times \text{ distance}$$

Here $r = -0.61$. Although 0.61 is rather low, because of the relative high $N = 22$ we can conclude that the relationship can be considered as linear. But, of course, this does not exclude better fits by using other functions such as

$$y = ax^b$$

With $b = -2.945$, we find a nonlinear relation and the fit is now much better (using a package for nonlinear regression; we do not discuss this here).

12. Exercise 12 with regression line

$$y = 244.87 + 11.87t.$$

Here $r = 0.96$, again very high.

Conclusion

We hope you have found this book interesting and that it will prove helpful to you in the (near) future. Our aim has been to provide useful insights into how quite simple statistical manipulations can add authority and informational value to library data. This will ensure that your reports will be based on facts, not just beliefs and opinions.

The confident and correct use of statistics is especially valuable in discussions with administrators and civil servants, who will appreciate being spoken to by real professionals using the appropriate statistical language. This may have appreciable benefits for library funding. Other occupational groups may, moreover, gain a better understanding of the important role of library and information service management.

For readers who would like to explore the subject in greater depth, useful introductory statistical texts abound. These books describe a wide range of other statistical tests, such as goodness-of-fit tests (often chi-squared tests), how to fit curves in general (not only linear relations), how to find relations between several variables acting as possible causes for an observed phenomenon (multivariate statistics), and so on. Texts covering these subjects are also freely available on the internet.

Library managers and network planners must know in some detail how users react to the stimuli offered by the library environment. On the basis of this knowledge, and with the help of a general mathematical model they will be able to predict future use of library facilities and make appropriate decisions. The field that studies such models and that provides guidelines in formulating the resulting decisions is known as operational research. Linear programming, a technique for the optimum allocation of scarce resources, is probably the best-known method applied in this field. One could say that statistics and operational research are the two pillars on which library management, as a science, is founded. The book *Operations Research for Libraries and Information Agencies: Techniques for the Evaluation of Management Decision Alternatives* by Donald H. Kraft and Bert R. Boyce (San Diego, Academic Press, 1991) offers the interested reader an excellent introduction to this subject.

Books, especially research books in fast developing fields, tend to become obsolete very quickly; however, we hope that this book, being of a quite different nature, will - just like your favourite cookery book - last a lifetime.

Appendix 1: Table of random numbers

94015	46874	32444	48277	59820	96163	64654	25843	41145	42820
74108	88222	88570	74015	25704	91035	01755	14750	48968	38603
62880	87873	95160	59221	22304	90314	72877	17334	39283	04149
11748	12102	80580	41867	17710	59621	06554	07850	73950	79552
17944	05600	60478	03343	25852	58905	57216	39618	49856	99326
66067	42792	95043	52680	46780	56487	09971	59481	37006	22186
54244	91030	45547	70818	59849	96169	61459	21647	87417	17198
30945	57589	31732	57560	47670	07654	46376	25366	94746	49580
69170	37403	86995	90307	94304	71803	26825	05511	12459	91314
08345	88975	35841	85771	08105	59987	87112	21476	14713	71181
27767	43584	85301	88977	29490	69714	73035	41207	74699	09310
13025	14338	54066	15243	47724	66733	47431	43905	31048	56699
80217	36292	98525	24335	24432	24896	43277	58874	11466	16082
10875	62004	90391	61105	57411	06368	53856	30743	08670	84741
54127	57326	26629	19087	24472	88779	30540	27886	61732	75454
60311	42824	37301	42678	45990	43242	17374	52003	70707	70214
49739	71484	92003	98086	76668	73209	59202	11973	02902	33250
78626	51594	16453	94614	39014	97066	83012	09832	25571	77628
66692	13986	99837	00582	81232	44987	09504	69412	90193	79568
44071	28091	07362	97703	76447	42537	98524	97831	65704	09514
41468	85149	49554	17994	14924	39650	95294	00556	70481	06905
94559	37559	49678	53119	70312	05682	66986	34099	74474	20740
41615	70360	64114	58660	90850	64618	80620	51790	11436	38072
50273	93113	41794	86861	24781	89683	55411	85667	77535	99892
41396	80504	90670	08289	40902	05069	95083	06783	28102	57816

25807	24280	71529	78920	72682	07385	90726	57166	98884	08583
06170	97965	88302	98041	21443	41808	68984	83620	89747	98882
60808	54444	74412	81105	01176	28838	36421	16489	18059	51061
80940	44893	10408	36222	80582	71944	92638	40333	67054	16067
19516	90120	46759	71643	13177	55292	21036	82808	77501	97427
49386	54480	23604	23554	21785	41101	91178	10174	29420	90438
06312	88940	15995	69321	47458	64809	98189	81851	29651	84215
60942	00307	11897	92674	40405	68032	96717	54244	10701	41393
92329	98932	78284	46347	71209	92061	39448	93136	25722	08564
77938	63574	31384	51924	85561	29671	58137	17820	22751	36518
38101	77756	11657	13897	95889	57067	47648	13885	70669	93406
39641	69457	91339	22502	92613	89719	11947	56203	19324	20504
84054	40455	99396	63680	67667	60631	69181	96845	38525	11600
47468	03577	57649	63268	24700	71594	14004	23153	69249	05747
43321	31370	28977	23898	76479	68562	62342	07589	08899	05985
64281	61826	18555	64937	13173	33365	78851	16499	87064	13075
66847	70495	32350	02685	86716	38746	26313	77463	55387	72681
72461	33230	21529	53424	92581	02262	78438	66276	18396	73538
21032	91050	13058	16218	12470	56500	15292	76139	59526	52113
95362	67011	06651	16136	01016	00857	55018	56374	35824	71708
49712	97380	10404	55452	34030	60726	75211	10271	36633	68424
58275	61764	97586	54716	50259	46345	87195	46092	26787	60939
89514	11788	68224	23417	73959	76145	30342	40277	11049	72049
15472	50669	48139	36732	46874	37088	73465	09819	58869	35220
12120	86124	51247	44302	60883	52109	21437	36786	49226	77837

Appendix 2: Logic of calculations

First $\times$ and $\div$ (there is no priority between $\times$ and $\div$; any order will do) then $+$ and $-$ (there is no priority between $+$ and $-$; any order will do). Use of brackets $(\ldots)$ gives priority to the calculations inside the brackets.

Examples

$5 \times 3 + 2 : 4 = 15.5$

$5 \times (3 + 2) : 4 = 6.25$

$5 \times (3 + 2 : 4) = 17.5$

Exercises

Calculate with a pocket calculator (see also Appendix 3 describing universal keys on a pocket calculator).

1. $(3 + 5) - (7 - 4) = 5$

2. $3^2 - 2^2 = 5$

3. $3^{2.5} - 2^{2.5} = 9.932$

4. $\left(\dfrac{1}{10^{1.5}} + 3.2^{2.7} \right) 7.1 = 138.63$

5. $\sqrt{((5.1 - 4.2)3.2 - 0.4)^2 + 3.25} = 3.066$

6. $((\sqrt{2} - \sqrt{1.5})^2 + 1.5)4^{2.5} = 49.149$

Note that all $\cdot$ denote decimals. The multiplication sign $\times$ is omitted in combination with brackets.

Appendix 3: Basic arithmetic on pocket calculators

No matter how powerful and cheap personal computers may become, there will always be a need for a pocket calculator. Indeed, for simple arithmetic operations pocket calculators are faster and easier to use. They are relatively cheap and can be used anywhere.

Note that computers usually have a calculator utility, which performs the same operations as a pocket calculator.

There are basically two ways of performing arithmetic operations on a calculator: one based on the usual mathematical notation, and one based on the Polish notation (this system is used by Hewlett-Packard calculators). We begin by explaining the first and simplest method. (Note, though, that some types of calculators may have keys that differ slightly from the ones described here.)

Here the $\boxed{+}$, $\boxed{-}$, $\boxed{\times}$, $\boxed{:}$ and $\boxed{=}$ keys are used as in primary school mathematics, so one presses the keys as follows:

681 $\boxed{\times}$ 27 $\boxed{=}$ and the result is shown as $18\,387$.

Combinations of these elementary operations are possible, as described in Appendix 2. Other keys are

$\boxed{\sqrt{x}}$ the square root key

$\boxed{x^2}$ the square key

Usually these keys are combined on one button:

9 $\boxed{\sqrt{x}}$ shows 3;

4 $\boxed{x^2}$ shows 16.

For one of these operations, use the "second function" key $\boxed{2nd}$

The key $\boxed{1/x}$ means: 1 divided by the number you key in.

An example: 9 $\boxed{1/x}$ gives 0.1111...

5 $\boxed{y^x}$ 3 gives $5^3 = 125$

Finally, the $\boxed{+/-}$ key reverses the sign:
an example: $5 \boxed{+/-}$ yields -5.

In the system based on the Polish notation there is one big difference: the $=$ is not present (at least not in the sense used above). To perform addition, subtraction, multiplication and division one has to do the following:

$5 \boxed{\text{ENTER}}\ 7 \boxed{\text{ENTER}}\ \boxed{+}$: this yields the sum of 5 and 7, which is 12.

Similarly,

$5 \boxed{\text{ENTER}}\ 7 \boxed{\text{ENTER}}\ \boxed{-}$ gives -2

$5 \boxed{\text{ENTER}}\ 7 \boxed{\text{ENTER}}\ \boxed{\times}$ gives 35

$5 \boxed{\text{ENTER}}\ 7 \boxed{\text{ENTER}}\ \boxed{:}$ gives $0.714285....$

Appendix 4: List of notation

Symbol	Explanation	Page of definition or of first use
Ω	universe	10
(x, y)	abscissa and ordinate	23
$y = f(x)$	y is a function of x	23
$y = a + bx$	general equation of a straight line	24
b	slope	24
a	intercept	24
t	time	24
$[x, y[$	half open interval	26
$[x, y]$	closed interval	29
$\bar{x}$	average or mean	41
N	number of elements under consideration; also sample size	41
$\sum_{i=1}^{N} x_i$	summation	41
s^2	variance	43
s	standard deviation	44
P_j	jth percentile	45
Q_i	ith quartile	45
Md	median	45
G	geometric mean	48
H	harmonic mean	49
V	variation coefficient	49
μ	population mean	58
Z	standardised normal variable	61
$1 - P$	degree of confidence	62
α	length of a confidence interval	80
θ	fraction of the mean	81
$\prod_{i=1}^{k} x_i$	product	95
r	correlation coefficient	96
x^b	power function	100

Bibliography

Almind, T.C. and Ingwersen, P. (1997). Informetric analyses on the world wide web: methodological approaches to "webometrics". *Journal of Documentation*, 53, 404–426.

ARL Statistics. Association of Research Libraries. Washington D.C.. ISSN 0147–2135.

Baglow, G. and Bottle, R.T. (1979). Rate of publication of British chemists. *Chemistry in Britain*, 15, 138–141.

Beltaos, L. and Rousseau, R. (1996). Some remarks concerning misshelved books. *JISSI, the International Journal of Scientometrics and Informetrics*, 2, 17–20

Buckland, M.K., Hindle, A. and Walker, G.P.M. (1975). Methodological problems in assessing overlap between bibliographical files and library holdings. *Information Processing and Management*, 11, 89–105.

Cleveland, W.S. (1985). *The Elements of Graphing Data*. Wadsworth, Monterey (CA, USA).

Cleveland, W.S. and McGill, R. (1984). Graphical perception: theory, experimentation, and application to the development of graphical methods. *Journal of the American Statistical Association*, 79, 531–554.

Egghe, L. (2000). New informetric aspects of the Internet: some reflections – many problems. *Journal of Information Science*, 26, 329–335.

Egghe, L. and Rousseau, R. (1990). *Introduction to Informetrics. Quantitative Methods in Library, Documentation and Information Science*. Elsevier, Amsterdam.

Egghe, L., Rousseau, R. and Van Hooydonk, G. (2000). Methods for accrediting publications to authors or countries: Consequences for evaluation studies. *Journal of the American Society for Information Science*, 51, 145–157.

Egghe, L. and Veraverbeke, N. (1995). Confidence intervals and sample sizes for multinomial data. *JISSI, the International Journal of Scientometrics and Informetrics*, 1, 183–193.

Fussler, H. and Simon, J. (1961). *Patterns in the Use of Books in Large Research Libraries*. University of Chicago Press, Chicago.

Howarth, R.J. and Turner, M.S.J. (1987). Statistical graphics in geochemical journals. *Mathematical Geology*, 19, 1–24.

ISO (1991). Information and documentation – statistiques internationales de bibliothèques. UNESCO, Genève.

Johnson, R.A. and Wichern, D.W. (1988). *Applied Multivariate Statistical Analysis*. Prentice–Hall, London.

Lied, T.R. and Tolliver, D.L. (1974). A general statistical model for increasing efficiency and confidence in manual data collection systems through sampling. *Journal of the American Society for Information Science*, 25, 327–331.

Lowenberg, S. (1989). A comprehensive shelf reading program. *Journal of Academic Librarianship*, 15(1), 24–27.

Marchionini, G. and Maurer, H. (1995). The roles of digital libraries in teaching and learning. *Communications of the ACM*, 38(4), 67–75.

Menzul, F. (1993). Use of information service statistics for communications with management. *Bulletin of the American Society for Information Science*, 19(2), 21–22.

Miller, B. and Sorum, M. (1977). A two stage sampling procedure for estimating the proportion of lost books in a library. *The Journal of Academic Librarianship*, 3, 74–80.

Morse, P.M. (1968). *Library Effectiveness: a Systems Approach*. MIT University Press, Cambridge (MA, USA).

Poll, R. and te Boekhorst, P. (1996). Measuring Quality. International Guidelines for Performance Measurement in academic Libraries. IFLA Section on University Libraries and other General Research Libraries. K.G. Saur, München.

Ramsdale, P. (1987). A Study of Library Economics in the European Communities. C.E.E. (Information Management) LIB1−ECON.

Rousseau, R. (1992). Concentration and diversity of availability and use in information systems: a positive reinforcement model. *Journal of The American Society for Information Science*, 43(5), 391−395.

Rousseau, R. and Vandegehuchte, P. (1995). Books and their users: socio-cultural and linguistic aspects in an engineering school. *Library Science with a Slant to Documentation and Information Studies*, 32, 143−150.

SCONUL (1992). Performance Indicators for University Libraries. SCONUL, London.

UNESCO (1989). UNESCO Questionnaire on statistics of libraries: Part II: libraries of institutions of higher education and school libraries in 1987, Paris.

Ward, S., Sumsion, J., Fuegi, D. and Bloor, I. (1995). Library Performance Indicators and Library Management Tools. Libraries in the Information Society, European Commission DG XIII − E3, Brussels.

Subject Index